UP AGAINST IT

Dedication
To my wife Kate
and to my children Sharon and Nigel
and my son-in-law Gerry
and to the parents I never had the chance to know.

Up Against It

Martin James

The Crowood Press

First published in 1994 by
The Crowood Press Ltd
Ramsbury, Marlborough
Wiltshire SN8 2HR

© Martin James 1994

British Library Cataloguing-in-Publication Data
A catalogue record for this book is available from the British Library.

ISBN 1 85223 792 9

Typeset by Acorn Bookwork, Salisbury, Wiltshire
Printed in Great Britain by Redwood Books, Trowbridge, Wiltshire

Contents

Foreword

---

by

Lady Clitheroe

Although I am no angler myself, I appreciate the joy that the sport provides for countless anglers the world over.

Not only is Martin James a man who has experienced the true pleasures of his sport in many countries, but he has the skill to write about it and give others some feeling for its thrills and delights.

Martin is also an example to us all of a man who has the resilience and stamina to overcome dreadful afflictions and still remain full of vitality and fun. His work for charity, and in particular the Crossroads Carers Organization, deserves outstanding praise.

Anyone who is even marginally interested in angling and field sports will derive great pleasure from this book, which I heartily commend.

Juliet Clitheroe

Acknowledgements

I should like to thank the following people who helped me while I was writing this book: Mark and Jackie Williams for their encouragement and their kindness in letting me use their beautiful thirteenth century cottage where much of the book was written; Pat and Adrienne O'Reilly for teaching me to use a word processor and helping me to put my stories into this book; Bernard and Eileen Venables for help with things from the past, and the lovely suppers; Neil Smith of Northampton who phones every week to see how things are, and sends me books and bits and pieces of old tackle; Richard and Sue Carter who made me some classic centre-pin reels; Alan Bramley of Partridge of Redditch who has kept me supplied with the best hooks in the world; Derek and Sheila Hoskin; Dr Smith and the staff at the Clitheroe Health Centre who have kept me going; the people of the Ribble Valley who adopted me and helped me through the rough times; and fellow anglers, wildfowlers and naturalists too numerous to mention.

These days I use split bamboo rods for a lot of my fishing and, knowing about my love of old tackle, some of my listeners have sent me rods and centre-pin reels. To all of them, a special thank you.

To Ron, Tom, Mick, Len, Chris, John, Janet, Carol and Avril: thanks for being my brothers and sisters; and didn't we have the best Mum and Dad in the world? And finally I must thank my wife and fishing companion, Kate, who has been at my side with love, help and encouragement over the past four years and has supplied me with endless cups of tea during the writing of this book.

CHAPTER 1

Battling with Multiple Sclerosis

The Four Seasons

The bite of winter, the glow of spring,
These are what the seasons bring.
The summer sun, the autumn shades,
Create a year of changing days.
See the beauty in each one;
Make the most before it's gone.
Watch how nature paints anew,
Every year, the seasons true.

Lorraine Davies

In 1976 I was told I had multiple sclerosis. An incurable, progressive disease . . . the end of the world? Well, for me it very nearly was. I assumed there was nothing I could do about it, and I let myself fall into a black pit of depression, self-pity and despair. I could so easily have stayed there – I might have died there in abject misery – but by some miracle I was pulled out to build a new life and, as it turned out, a rewarding and enjoyable one.

So what happened? Well, for several years I had been having problems with pins and needles in my arms and legs. At times my speech was slurred and my hands were numb and by midday all I wanted to do was sleep. My GP had sent me to hospital where, after many tests, I was given a course of drugs. My condition seemed to improve. Many of the symptoms even disappeared for a while, although I still suffered badly from pins and needles in my hands, and occasionally I would fall over for no apparent reason. Up to this time I had been as fit as a butcher's dog.

In 1975 I started having serious problems: I was dragging my left leg and getting double and blurred vision. Around this time my brother Mick was diagnosed as having MS, and our mother was dying with cancer. Trying desperately to hold down a new job, I was not a happy man. It was even difficult to go fishing, because some days I couldn't hold a pen, never mind a fishing rod. Something was wrong . . . but what?

I was sent to see the late Professor Liversedge in Manchester. He told me,

3

'We'll soon find out what is wrong with you, young man.' I left feeling he would sort me out whatever the problem. I was admitted to Burnley General Hospital, where the doctors and nurses were marvellous. Thank goodness we have a National Health Service – although I do worry these days about what is happening to the NHS, with all the cutbacks and threats of privatization.

I was given a lumbar puncture, which was really painful. Then I had several more; how I hated them! I worried about what was wrong with me, all the while fearing that it might be cancer. Another of the patients had been diagnosed as having a brain tumour, and his symptoms were the same as mine. He was to die a few weeks later. I had plenty of time to worry, because I was in hospital for many long weeks. To make matters worse, my mother died while I was there and I couldn't even attend the funeral.

One Friday afternoon Mr Watson, the consultant, came round the ward. He talked to all the patients, sending some home but deciding that others would have to stay. One man, a heavy smoker who was in because of a heart attack, said, 'What's been the matter with me, doctor?'

There was a pause and then Mr Watson said, 'You've had a fall of soot.'

We all chuckled at that.

Then it was my turn. The doctors, nurses and Mr Watson all gathered round my bed and the curtains were pulled. I thought, 'This is it. . .'

The consultant asked how I felt.

What can you say at such a time? I just said, 'Not too bad. But what's wrong with me?'

He just stood there, looking at my notes, so I said, 'You can tell me. It's me that needs to know.'

Quietly he said, 'I'm sorry to say you have multiple sclerosis.'

'Thanks very much. Now I know what I have to fight.'

'Do you know what MS is?' he asked.

'Yes,' I told him. 'My brother was diagnosed with it a couple of months ago. I can't walk but that doesn't matter. Douglas Bader fought the Germans with tin legs; I only want to catch a few fish.'

We had a chat, and then I asked, 'Can I go home for the weekend?'

He said, 'Yes. Saturday lunchtime to Sunday evening,' and he went on his way.

I pulled the covers over my face and had a good weep. I was devastated. At that moment I just wanted to die.

Coming to my senses I phoned Mike Harris down in Kent and told him the bad news. Mike travelled from Kent to Lancashire on the Saturday so I could spend a few hours out of hospital. We went across to Roy Worrell's family in Manchester for the Sunday, and then Mike dropped me off at the hospital before heading home to Kent – a round trip of over 600 miles. When in trouble you certainly find out who your friends are. Mike had to be the best.

A few days later I was told that I could go home. Home to what? I thought.

No fishing. No shooting. I was a prisoner, but one who had committed no crime. What sort of life could I have without fishing?

I was fitted up with a wheelchair, and as I was being wheeled out to the ambulance I overheard one nurse say to another, 'I feel sorry for that man. He won't ever walk again.'

I stopped the wheelchair and, turning to the nurses, said, 'Don't you worry about that! I'll walk again, and when I do I'll come and take you out for dinner!' Five years later, when I was more mobile, I went back to the hospital. One of the nurses, whose name was Mary, was still working there. We had a long chat, and later that week, Mary, her husband and I went out for dinner together.

All those weeks in hospital were tough, but my problems *really* started when I arrived home. I couldn't get up the stairs – in fact it was difficult getting around the room even on a so-called good day. I had to live in the lounge twenty-four hours a day, seven days a week. Even prisoners are allowed out of their cells for exercise, but for me there was no escape and no exercise.

I became really depressed, even suicidal, but didn't have the means for the job. Sometimes I would go to sleep at night with red-rimmed eyes from crying, wishing I wouldn't wake up. I used to say, 'Why me? Why have I got MS?' I was bedridden for weeks at a time, and it was a relief on the days when I could drag myself from my bed to my wheelchair and sit out in the garden.

I was put on different drugs, and a nurse would call every morning to get me washed, dressed and shaved; this I hated, so I decided to grow a beard. I got progressively worse. People would call to see me, offering help, but there was no help they could give. The local bobby used to drop in and tell me who was catching what. My weight went up to over seventeen stone owing to a combination of the drugs, no exercise and eating lots of sweet things. I had a craving for anything sweet and I would eat a jar of honey or a tin of golden syrup in a day. I smoked continuously. I wasn't doing myself any favours!

The social services were wonderful. My social worker, Roy Morris, was an angler and that helped. He arranged for another room to be built on to the back of the house, with a shower unit and a toilet; at least then I had a room to myself. I was having bouts when my whole body would shake and I was in so much pain that I wanted to scream. One day I couldn't see, and thought I had gone blind; I could just make out the blurred window. The doctor was called; she was such a pleasant person, and said, 'Don't worry. The combination of your MS and the very hot weather has caused the problem.' She was right, thank goodness: a couple of days later my sight came back.

While I was bedridden my father died in a house fire. It seemed there was no end to my troubles! I suppose I had about three years of this purgatory, being a prisoner through no fault of my own.

I was visiting the hospital regularly, and one day the consultant said, 'I don't want to see you any more.'

'Why not?' I asked.

'Because you undo all our good work by smoking.'

'All right,' I said. 'I won't smoke any more, then.'

'You're like all the rest. You won't be able to pack it up.'

'Yes I will,' I said firmly. 'Just give me a try.'

He did, and from that day I never smoked again.

This, I believe, was the turning point. A challenge had been thrown down, and all my life I had relished challenges. Two weeks later I was back at the hospital to have a good chat with the consultant. He listened while I poured out my troubles, and then he said, 'I understand how you feel. But remember how you once told me that if Douglas Bader could fight the Germans with a pair of tin legs you could fight a few fish? Go and give it a try. I would like you to catch me a trout.'

Next time the local bobby called I said, 'Can you get me down to the Rochdale canal for a few hours fishing?'

'No problem,' he told me. 'When do you want to go?'

'Tomorrow!'

We chatted, and after he left I picked up *Stillwater Angling* by Richard Walker – he was fighting a battle with cancer at the time – and lost myself in the book for a couple of hours. Tomorrow I was going fishing!

My life soon became more satisfying. I was being taken to the waterside once or twice a week, and I decided to try and get to the back gate with a walking frame. Everyone told me I had no chance, but I said, 'I don't care what you all say, I'm *going to do it*.'

A HELPING HAND

It was easier said than done: two steps and I would crash over. I would pick myself up, throwing the frame across the room or punching the floor in anger and frustration. *Why* couldn't I walk? I must have asked myself that question a thousand times. Once I made it as far as the kitchen, but it seemed that, even with all my will-power, I just couldn't win. Then my friend Marlene, who was a nurse, said, 'I'll give you a hand. Between us we'll crack it.'

For over six months, with Marlene's help I tried, unsuccessfully, to walk a few feet with a frame. Then it happened. Marlene said, 'Come on. I'm taking you down to the canal for a few hours.'

I sorted out some tackle, and then Marlene said, 'Grab that frame of yours, and let's go. The wheelchair's in the car.'

Without thinking, I pulled myself up on the frame and, with hesitant steps, waddled to the car at the back gate. It was only when I was in the car that I realized what I had done. I threw my arms around Marlene, gave her a kiss and said, 'I've done it!'

Marlene told me later that she thought I would only be able to do it if I didn't think about it. From then on there was light at the end of the tunnel.

CENTRE OF ATTENTION

One day my social worker asked, 'Have you thought about going to Temple Street Physically Handicapped Centre?'

I said, 'No, mate. What's there for me? I'm no use to anyone.'

'Well, why don't you come down for a day and have a look around?' he insisted.

I agreed to go, and the next morning the ambulance picked me up, along with a couple of other people in wheelchairs. Off we went.

Everyone at the Centre was very friendly, some of them far worse off than me. Some were blind; others, like me, were in wheelchairs; one man had no legs, having lost them when his Spitfire crash-landed in the desert during the war. I watched him jump around the floor on a piece of leather. He told me he did a bit of fishing, enjoyed a drop of whisky, and had a few girlfriends. It is truly amazing how some people cope with disability.

I had lunch with everyone and then went home at tea time. I enjoyed my day, so I kept going back to the Centre: it took me out of my prison. The barber called each week, and sometimes one of the carers would help me into the bath – up until then it had been showers for me.

It was about this time that I acquired an electric wheelchair. Now I could go out on my own, and summer or winter I would be out and about in Burnley. I had a favourite café where I went on Saturdays, and if it was cold or wet I visited the library, spending hours in the reference section. However, if I travelled too far from home, the batteries would die on me, and then it was a case of asking someone to phone the Centre to pick me up in the ambulance. The AA, the police and numerous members of the public have all run me home late at night. For wet weather I had a cape which fitted over me and the wheelchair, so I was quite comfortable. I even went shooting in that electric wheelchair and, because the motor was quiet, it was a doddle to creep along a hedgerow at dawn or dusk and surprise the rabbits. We enjoyed many a rabbit pie that way!

For six years I continued to visit the Temple Street Centre regularly. It was my sanctuary, a place where I could forget my problems, and I shall always think of the Centre with great affection. It was, I believe, my salvation.

GOING FOR GOLD

Thursday evening was games night at the Centre. We played table tennis and snooker, and did wheelchair dancing – in fact I discovered there's not much you can't do if you put your mind to it. The staff at the Centre were wonderful: nothing was too much trouble. Each day the ambulance drivers would come and pick me up, and they always had a cheerful word.

Bill Lofthouse, who was chairman of the Centre's sports section, asked if anyone wanted to take part in the disabled games in Bolton. I thought, 'In for a penny, in for a pound,' and put my name down for table tennis, discus, shot and javelin. I chose these events because you build up strong arm muscles pushing a wheelchair. I won a gold and two silver medals which I gave to my children Sharon and Nigel.

After this initial success I put everything I had into events up and down the country, culminating in the disabled games at Stoke Mandeville where I represented the North West. There I set a new national record in the javelin, picking up a gold medal. I also won silvers in the discus and the shot, in each case missing the gold by just a few centimetres.

Also in 1983 I won the National Angling Championship of the British Sports Association for the Disabled. The match was held at Rickmansworth, and Gladys Whittaker, manageress of Temple Street Centre, drove me to the event and sorted out the overnight accommodation. I gave my prize of a bottle of champagne to Gladys, and the trophy to the Centre.

Table tennis was another game in which I became seriously involved. We disabled players were in the third division of the Burnley and District League, and were coached by Bob Wright, one of the top local players. We played all our matches at home, but the only other concession made to us was that in the mixed doubles we were allowed to play the ball according to which court we were in (as in lawn tennis) rather than alternating. I gave it everything I had, but could never win. I might take the first leg 21–15 only to lose the next two, but it was great fun.

One evening we sat chatting in the Centre. One of the members asked if we could have some carpet bowls. The answer was no; there wasn't the money.

'Don't worry about that,' I said. 'We'll raise the money.'

'How?' Bill Lofthouse asked.

'I'll do a sponsored wheelchair fish-in,' I told him.

Bernie Calvert, of the Hollies pop group, gave us permission to use his lake for the event. Working with Walter Wade, a senior probation officer from Haslingdon, Gladys helped get the thing off the ground. I fished from 29 September to 2 October, a total of seventy-six hours. It was terribly hard to stay awake but many people helped me, including members of the local police force and fire brigade who came to keep me company. Gladys would turn up at around 10 p.m. with a couple of hot-water bottles, and then at dawn with bacon sandwiches. The local newspapers and radio covered the event and encouraged people to donate their pennies and pounds. It worked: we raised over £850, and Temple Street had its carpet bowls.

FISHING FROM A WHEELCHAIR

I was back to fishing in a big way: for trout in the International Disabled Fly Fishing Championships at Rutland Water, where I had second highest individual weight; for rudd and bream in Ireland; for roach and barbel on the Kennet and the Dorset Stour. I was back doing the things I loved best – I even went wildfowling in Scotland. It was a case of 'Have wheelchair, will travel'!

The wheelchair, however, almost became the instrument of my death. It happened on the Wharfe, a Yorkshire spate river where I was fishing in chest waders. My mate had pushed me and my wheelchair out onto a gravel bar near the middle of the river so that I could trot my bait down a deep channel, searching for chub and roach; then he had gone off downstream to another swim. I was quite content, catching some nice chub and roach, when I noticed that the water had changed to a dirty brown colour. Twigs and leaves were floating down. The water was rising and my wheelchair was beginning to rock. There must have been rain in the hills. Suddenly I felt the chair inch forward. I was in real trouble!

Three yards below me the water was ten feet deep. Don't panic, I told myself. Think it out. I did, and soon worked out that I was going to drown. I shouted – no, I screamed – for my mate, but got no answer. Soon the water was up to my chest.

At the side of the river was a lane, a favourite stopping point for lorry drivers, and at that moment a driver got out of his cab and shouted, 'Are you okay?'

'No,' I screamed back. 'I'm drowning. I can't get out!'

The lorry driver was over the wall in a flash and sliding down the bank. Wading waist deep into the river, he grabbed my wheelchair and hauled me back to safety.

'That was a bloody silly thing to do,' he told me.

'But I did catch some good fish.'

'Yes, and nearly drowned yourself in the process,' he said.

After that I always made sure that someone was close at hand when I was fishing from my wheelchair in the river.

This driver had his work to do, of course. I asked him his name, but he just wanted to get going. 'Don't worry about that,' he said, and he jumped up into his cab and was away. However, I made a mental note of the name of his firm, which was based in Bradford, and sent a letter asking them to thank the driver for what he had done. I later discovered that he had been given a reward by his company, and that he had donated the money to the Multiple Sclerosis Society. Thankfully there are still a few nice people in the world!

STRUGGLES AND SETBACKS

Multiple Sclerosis affects people in different ways. Some soon become permanently bedridden; others have symptoms for a short time and then appear to get over the disease completely; many more, like myself, have good times and bad times. It is always a struggle for me to get going in the mornings, but when my MS is at its worst I can be really bad for days or even weeks. That's the trouble with MS: setbacks can come without any warning.

For example, I used to fish a lake in Gloucestershire, and very good fishing it was too. I'm pretty certain I spotted a roach of 4lb, and there was definitely a tench well into double figures. Many times I had this huge fish in my swim, but no way would it pick up a bait. Each year I would spend three or four weeks camping on the banks of this lake, and then one night I was going back to my bivvy after a cuppa with Dick Cator, the bailiff, when I blacked out and fell down the bank. Coming to at the water's edge in total darkness, I found that I couldn't move. I tried to call Dick but couldn't utter a sound, and so I had to spend a cold and miserable night lying there. In the morning, on his way round to my bivvy with a paper and some milk, Dick found me. I was in a terrible state. He dragged me back to the bivvy, and that's where I stayed for three days just lying on my camp bed. Dick looked after me, cooking meals and making tea, and telling me about his life in the RAF.

Another time my friend, Derek Green, helped me out when I had a bad spell. I had just been fishing the River Bure for pike when I collapsed with an attack of the shakes; I felt freezing cold and couldn't talk. Derek rescued me, taking me back to his caravanette where he tucked me up in a warm sleeping bag and gave me a hot meal. Next morning he took me home, and so that was the end of that fishing trip.

Although nowadays there are times when I am confined to my wheelchair and with all the will in the world there is nothing I can do about it, most days I can get about with my walking frame, and quite often I manage without it; so I count myself quite lucky.

CHAPTER 2

Early Days

_____

1939–1945

When the sound of sirens filled you with fear,
And the throbbing of planes was so close and so clear,
And the lights were snuffed out, and a black curtain hung,
And we all wondered why such a war had begun;
When doodlebugs made a terrible noise,
And the loss of young lives and families destroyed
Are the pages of history we now look back to,
Yet we still can recall a joy that we knew
In the sharing and caring; then together, with pride,
Found the passage of victory soothed the tears that we'd cried.

Lorraine Davies

As an only child I was unconventional: I had more than two hundred brothers and sisters; but then I had two mothers and fathers. My first father, Rodney Stewart Martin James-McGregor, came from Aberdeen. He was an officer in the navy, and so my mother, who had been a nurse, was able to have her baby in Canada House nursing home. There in Gillingham, south of the Medway, I was born on 27 October 1937. This made me a man of Kent; had I been born north of the Medway I would have been known as a Kentish man. I spent little time with my parents who were often overseas, but I had a nanny who was to become my mother four years later when my parents were killed in the war in the Far East.

I feel that I really started life in 1941, which was when I became an angler. Then Britain stood alone against Hitler's Nazi Germany, and our brave men and women were fighting for freedom in many places throughout the world. My lovely county of Kent, the Garden of England, was in the front line in the battle against Nazism. Day after day, night after night we were bombed and strafed as our ack-ack batteries and fighter planes struggled to beat off the invaders. Most of my adoptive family were serving in the forces.

School was often interrupted by air-raid warnings and bombings. By day, dog fights between German and British fighters were a common sight, with parachutists floating earthwards among the barrage balloons, and, at night, searchlights from Lodgehill pierced the skies, seeking enemy planes on their way to bomb London. Khaki-clad soldiers were everywhere, on exercise, operating ack-ack guns, searchlights and smoke screens, aboard tanks, armoured cars and lorries, some, perhaps, on their way to battle in Europe, the Middle East or the Far East.

Most of the countryside was out of bounds to us children, but a sign saying *Private* was merely an invitation to go in and search for the relics of war; thoughts of danger never entered our innocent heads. What we hoped most of all to find was a piece of a German aircraft or shrapnel from a bomb. I collected empty .303 cases and army cap badges, most prized of which were those of the Royal West Kents, the Parachute Regiment and REME, as these were the regiments in which my family served.

To us youngsters war was a big adventure. We clapped, jumped and shouted when fighters flew across the rooftops heading skywards to take on Jerry. Lots of children who lived around me were evacuated to other parts of the country where it was considered to be safe, but my mother said, 'Hitler or not, we are all staying together'. And we did, all through the war, even when we got bombed out. At night we sat in the air-raid shelter watching the searchlights. The ground shook when the German bombs exploded around us, and when a bomb was very close we would get covered in dust and dirt which came through gaps where the roof of the Anderson shelter was bolted together. Everyone was most worried when incendiary bombs were falling; these were designed to cause fires, and after a heavy raid it looked as if the whole world was on fire. We had buckets of sand and a stirrup pump outside the house, but I don't really think they would have been much use against the incendiaries. Mum never seemed frightened; she used to say, 'Hitler won't win the war. They are the Fatherland and we are the Motherland, and Mother always has the last word!'

One night the Germans dropped bombs and landmines on the houses in and around Station Road. The landmines floated to earth on parachutes; unlike bombs they didn't cause craters but exploded at ground level. We were told they had tried to destroy Strood station and Rochester Bridge, but all they did was destroy lots of houses and kill several people there. A few days later I went down Station Road on my way to see my grandmother; the houses opposite Strood station were flattened and there was rubble everywhere. Some of the children from my school had been killed.

I lived on Frindsbury Hill, opposite the fish shop and the greengrocer. Just up the road was the Five Bells pub where my father, my uncles and aunts, and their army, navy and air force friends went when home on leave. As the war progressed, more and more Americans appeared, and my uncles would sometimes bring a couple of them to our house. It was good when they did: they gave us chocolates, biscuits and chewing gum, and sometimes I received a cap badge for my collection or was allowed to hold the bayonet which many seemed to wear all the time.

In the recreation ground across from where we lived there was an army smoke-screen unit and some air-raid shelters; sometimes my mother would take me over there so that I could talk to the soldiers. One day the air-raid warning sounded and we went down into their shelter, which was ever so big. I was also taken to see a barrage-balloon site manned by the Home Guard. I had a ride in one of the jeeps and watched the soldiers firing Sten guns – I wanted to fire guns when I got older. It was great fun, but despite all that, the wail of the siren was a fearsome sound and one that we, even as youngsters, knew heralded air raids which cost people their homes and perhaps their lives.

School was in the mornings only. One boy in our class did not like school and I had to collect him on my way. For this I got three pence a week.

One day my Uncle Fred came with me to school. He asked, 'Is that your teacher, there?' I nodded and Uncle Fred said, 'She's a smasher!' I told Miss Roberts what my Uncle Fred had said, and she blushed. For quite some time Uncle Fred came with me to school; then one day I heard Mum say to my Aunt Peg, 'Fred was up the Five Bells last night with that young school-teacher'. When I got back to school I told all the class, and one of the girls asked Miss Roberts if she was in love with a soldier. We had never seen our teacher go that colour before!

CRABBING, TIDDLERS AND MY MEADOW

A short distance from my home was Baker's Meadow, an oasis of peace and solitude set in the heart of the bombed and bullet-strafed Garden of England. Three acres of buttercups and daisies, the meadow was bordered on two sides by oak and elm trees. A deep narrow stream flowed slowly along the bottom of the meadow, while from the top a country lane led up to the ack-ack guns and searchlights on Lodgehill. Beyond the other side of the stream were the marshes and the River Medway. At high tide most of the marshes were covered, and in the summer mullet entered the creeks.

My mother and Aunt Peg used to take us down to Baker's Meadow for picnics. We made daisy chains, played hide-and-seek, and tried to play round-ers and cricket; but all the time I was drawn to the stream. To the best of my knowledge this stream only contained sticklebacks, small fish with spiny dorsal fins, and I spent many hours catching these with a home-made net fixed to a garden cane handle; then at home I would watch as these tiny fish swam round and round a 2lb jam jar until they died. Then fresh supplies would have to be captured.

In spring I had no trouble catching lots of tadpoles, but what I really wanted to do was to catch a proper fish using a rod and line like Grandad did on the canal at Higham. My Grandad did take me crabbing, however. We went to Strood pier where we used a piece of string with a nut or bolt as a weight. For bait we used snails broken from their shells. Sometimes we would catch as many as three crabs at a time, though most crabs would drop off as we lifted them from the water. Those we caught I would watch as they walked across the pier planking and fell into the sea with a splash. Occasionally there would be someone fishing with a rod and line, and then I wouldn't bother fishing for crabs but would watch this proper fisherman, hoping that I would be allowed to turn the handle of the reel and wind in a flatfish or an eel; being so small I couldn't manage the rod as well. It was terribly exciting.

FIRST FISH

Whenever he came home on leave I pestered my Uncle Len to take me fishing, but always the answer was, 'We can't. You haven't any tackle'. Then one day Mum said, 'Have this ball of wool and buy a hook from the ironmonger's, then you can go fishing'. I laughed, but accepted the wool. Uncle Len and I dug some worms and found some nuts in the shed (nuts as used on bolts). We bought some penny eel-hooks and then took the train from Strood.

The sun was shining as we left Higham station and headed for Cliffe marshes. We walked beside the old Higham canal which, my uncle told me, held rudd, tench and eels. It was a big adventure; I was going out to try to catch a real fish with a hook. After what seemed hours, sometimes walking, sometimes riding on my uncle's shoulders, we arrived at the clay pit. We found a gap in the reeds, then Uncle Len baited the hook with a worm and threw it out into the dark green water. I sat there, holding the line as Uncle Len told me to and we waited for something to happen. After what seemed like hours but was probably only minutes, I felt something tug on the line.

'Uncle Len,' I called, 'I've got a fish, I've got a fish!' As quickly as I could I pulled in the line. It seemed heavy. Then there it was: the most beautiful thing I had ever seen, my first fish, in my hand. Uncle Len said it was a rudd, and during that summer afternoon of 1941 I caught seven small rudd in all. I was an angler, and hooked for life.

Suddenly, a Hurricane roared across the tree tops and soared skywards towards some enemy aircraft. There was a fierce battle in the clear blue sky and soon we saw a German plane falling to earth and then a parachute. Uncle Len said, 'Come along, we must get the Home Guard so they can capture that German.'

'You go, Uncle, I want another fish. And I've got my jack-knife.' As if a knife would stop anyone from grabbing me! Most boys had jack-knives; mine had a black handle, a folding blade, a can-opener and a spike, and it was dated 1939. But Uncle Len would have none of it, and that was the end of my fishing for the day.

A few weeks later Uncle Len died, in the sands of North Africa, fighting Rommel's Afrika Korps. He had been top marksman in his regiment and had won many cups for shooting. But I shall never forget that wonderful afternoon of peace and tranquillity, until the war planes appeared: there I was, with one of my favourite uncles, on Cliffe marshes catching my first fish, when all around the world men were killing one another. But Uncle Len's love of fishing lives on in me to this day.

FIRST FISHING ROD

After that first day's proper fishing it was back to the tiddlers at Baker's Meadow and the crabs at Strood pier; but I kept thinking of those rudd at the clay pit. Time and again I asked Grandad to take me fishing there but all he ever said was, 'When you are older'. I didn't want to wait, and I pestered everyone who called at the house. Then I struck lucky: another uncle came home on leave from the Parachute Regiment. Uncle Eddy was a keen angler and had a brother who had a fishing rod and reel that I could have. It was a 9-foot rod in three pieces, the bottom two of cane and the top of lance wood; the tiny wooden reel was loaded with line as thick as string. That rod and reel became my pride and joy. Often I would take the rod out of its case and wipe it down with linseed oil splashed onto a cloth, just like Grandad had shown me.

In Rochester there was a pram shop next to the Majestic Picture Palace, and here I bought split shot in little tins with sliding lids; these were very sharp, and several times I cut my fingers trying to open them. I also bought a cardboard winder holding a length of silk line with a quill float and a hook tied to gut. Various relations gave me bits and pieces of tackle, and slowly my collection built up. But there were no fishing trips; all I could do was talk about fishing and hope that one day someone would take me. The trouble was, everyone was away at the war. My main hope was my grandfather on my father's side, because when he wasn't working as an air-raid warden or on his allotment, where he spent most of his time, he liked fishing – eels were his favourite; he liked to eat them after they had been jellied by Granny. Every time I saw him I pestered him to take me fishing. 'When the summer comes,' he would reply. It was always 'when the summer comes,' or 'you're not old enough yet,' or 'it's too far for you to walk.'

FISHING WITH GRANDAD AND UNCLE EDDY

When summer came Grandad did take me fishing. We went to Strood locks on the old canal and we fished for eels and Grandad caught a lot, which he put into a sack. But although I was allowed to reel one in occasionally, what I really wanted was to go back to Cliffe marshes after rudd, with my new rod and reel. But with Grandad it was the locks, Strood pier, or nothing. Then, just before D-Day in 1944, my Uncle Eddy and Fred Hepper came home on leave. Fred's son, Fred Hepper junior, was to win many awards for ballroom dancing in the 1950s and 1960s before becoming a Conservative councillor and later, Mayor of Medway Borough Council. Many years later I taught him and his young son, Gary, to fish.

Uncle Eddy took me fishing to a big old clay pit at the Alpha cement works on Cliffe marshes where there seemed to be millions of rudd, and they were easy to catch, even for a youngster. I used my new rod and reel, with worms as the bait, and it seemed that as soon as I cast into the murky water the float would disappear as a fish swallowed the worm, and I would reel in another small rudd. All too soon that exciting day was over, and my uncles were back in action on D-Day. For me it was back to Baker's Meadow with net and jam jar, or to Strood pier or the canal locks with my grandfather.

DOODLEBUGS

When the doodlebugs – V1 and V2 flying bombs – came over spitting flames from the back, we knew we were safe all the while we could hear the rocket motors. Doodlebugs were packed with explosives, and when the motor cut out it was bad news. One summer's day in 1944 we were playing in the back garden when the air-raid siren sounded. Mum shouted, 'All into the air-raid shelter!'

'No! Get in the house, under the table,' I shouted to my brothers and sisters.

We went and crouched under the big farmhouse table; Mum grabbed one of the children and took cover under the stairs. There was a huge bang, and the house shook as if the roof was falling in. It was. We were covered in dust, plaster, slates and what appeared to be millions of needles, which were in fact slivers of glass. Someone was crying; I think it was my little sister. I looked up at a gaping hole where the roof should have been, then scrambled around looking for my fishing rod. I found it in a dozen pieces. Tears welled up in my eyes, and I remember shouting, 'The Germans have broken my fishing rod'. When I had got all the children out of the house, a soldier appeared and

16

helped us across the road. Mum was in tears and was being comforted by one of the ARP wardens. We watched as the walls collapsed; we had got out in time but had lost nearly everything we owned. We never went back.

An amazing thing happened that day. Aunt Peg's baby daughter, Sylvia, was in her pram at the front of the house when a slate fell from the roof and penetrated the pram canopy, point on, coming to rest a couple of inches above her forehead. It was a miracle that she survived.

The ARP wardens and the fire brigade could do nothing. The air-raid shelter in the back garden had collapsed inwards and was reduced to rubble; had we been in there we would have been crushed to death. To this day I cannot tell you why I shouted, 'Everybody under the table in the kitchen!', but undoubtedly this saved our lives.

We salvaged a few clothes and made our way to Granny's house in Station Road where we stayed for a few weeks before moving to a house at Temple Farm on the outskirts of Strood. It was here that I first learned that my real mother and father had been killed; then the lady I had been calling 'Mum' adopted me after being told she couldn't have children of her own. But what a lovely mum she was! And she did eventually have her own children, two daughters, Janet and Carol, and four sons, Ron, Tom, Mick and Len; and she was later to adopt three others: Chris, John and Avril. She also fostered more than two hundred, some for two or three days, others for several months; the house was always full. Avril is now following in her footsteps and fostering children. Dad was very good and tried his best to give us most of the things we wanted, like fishing rods and cycles; I remember he even worked overtime one weekend to get the wood so that I could have a pigeon loft. They both gave me every encouragement, and although they had children of their own I felt that I received the lion's share of kindness. By today's standards I suppose we were quite poor, although we were better off than many of my friends because we had a bathroom and two toilets, one upstairs and one downstairs, and we had a wireless in the front room.

I loved listening to the wireless, especially *Dick Barton, Special Agent*, and *Paul Temple*, and we were allowed to listen to *Saturday Night Theatre* if we had behaved ourselves. I loved the comedy shows: *Much Binding in the Marsh, Life with the Lyons, Worker's Playtime, Jimmy Jewel and Ben Warris*, and the *Billy Cotton Band Show*. The wireless meant a lot to me then, and it still does today. I have always preferred to listen to sport on the wireless than to watch it on television.

Our wireless ran off an accumulator. Every Saturday one of us had to leave the accumulator at the cycle shop to be recharged and to collect the one we had left the week before. We had loudspeakers in two of the bedrooms, and in winter when it was very cold upstairs, with thick ice on the inside of the window panes, it was great to snuggle down in bed and listen to it.

CHICKENS FOR CHRISTMAS

Every January we bought between fifty and a hundred day-old chicks. To help keep them warm and well we used stone hot water bottles wrapped in flannel, and it was my job to keep the bottles filled with hot water. We also had a tea chest with an electric light bulb fixed in the top to give the chicks light and warmth. However, despite all our efforts many of them died and were fed to the ferrets; by the time they could manage on their own we had but a dozen or so to grow on for Christmas. We kept two or three for ourselves, and the rest we sold or raffled off to help pay for Christmas presents.

Springtime, I told my mates, meant slave labour: it was time to dig the garden and plant vegetables. We each had our jobs, and were not allowed out until they were done. I looked after the potatoes, lettuce, beetroot and cabbages. Dad liked to grow roses too and when the milkman came round I also had to go out with a bucket, shovel up the horse manure and put it round the roses. Woe betide me if a lad from another house got there first!

CHUB FOR A CUB

Like lots of boys I joined the Cubs, in my case the 1st St Mary's pack. What really tempted me was the promise of camping, and I put up with all the other things we used to do on Thursday evenings so that in the summer I could go to the River Medway at Wateringbury for a few days camp. There was an extra incentive too: while at camp Billy Race and I used to collect all the lemonade bottles from the river, wash them, and take them to the local shop for the deposits.

It was at camp that I caught my first chub. I had spotted some fish in the river and was determined to catch them, so I went up to the shop and bought a float winder with line, float and hook; for a rod I cut a branch from a tree. The Cub mistress gave me a piece of cheese, and with this I caught a small fish about eight inches long; a man fishing told me it was a chub. This was the first fish I ever caught from a river.

A summer treat was a trip on the *Medway Queen*. Although only a paddle steamer, she had taken part in the evacuation of thousands of troops from Dunkirk; my Uncle Len, who died in North Africa, was one of the men who returned from Dunkirk on the *Medway Queen* and I used to go to different parts of the ship wondering exactly where he had stood when he was being rescued in 1940. We went down the River Medway from Strood pier to Sheerness, on the Isle of Sheppey; there the family swam and played on the beach while I fished for eels with a handline from Sheerness pier. Sometimes I caught a dab or a flounder, and then I would jump with joy because this was a proper fish.

CYCLE TO FREEDOM

Until 1946 I had to be satisfied with fishing for crabs and eels, and then I had my first bicycle. It took me ten minutes to master the machine that was to be my passport to paradise. I was forbidden to go fishing on my own, but I did, making the excuse that I was going to visit Granny. I would go fishing in Cliffe marshes, the Higham canal or Leybourne Lake, always calling in to see Granny on the way home. The cycle was my ticket to angling freedom and adventure, and I loved every minute, even when I was wet and cold and had caught no fish.

Gordon Road junior school was a long way from home so I had to stay for school dinners. Some weeks I skipped dinners, taking my half-crown to Doughty's tackle shop in Rochester to buy bits and pieces of fishing tackle. Then, during the dinner hour, Mike Prudence and I would go off to the oil and cake mills to scrounge peanuts, or we would visit Granny who always found us something to eat. Ours was a mixed school, and in our class there was one girl, with long blond plaits, who was a real horror. One day when we were cutting and pasting things in a craft lesson our teacher shouted at me for scraping a chair along the floor, but that time it wasn't me. The snotty-nosed girl turned round and gave a wicked grin as if to say, 'Got you told off again' – and scraped her chair again.

'Who did that?' the teacher demanded, and this nasty little girl turned and pointed at me. Once more I was told off: but thirty seconds later her plaits had gone – I had chopped them off. All hell was let loose: I got caned, her mother had a go at my mother, and I got a clump from my father and was made to stay indoors all weekend. No fishing . . . but it was worth all that.

PLAYING HOOKY

I hated school, and our geography teacher in particular. So did Mike Prudence, and on Friday afternoons when it was geography I used to make myself sick by putting my fingers down my throat. Of course the teacher would get someone to take me home, and that someone was always Prudence. However, one day when Mike and I were playing hooky we got well and truly caught. While walking around the streets we met Mrs Brockwell, my next door neighbour; she asked what we were doing out of school and we tried to tell her that it was going home time. She pointed out that it was only three o'clock, and of course told my mother. I got a hiding from my father for that one, and had to stay in my bedroom for the weekend.

Another time a teacher, out on a nature ramble with a party of school children, caught me fishing in a pond. More trouble! My tackle was locked away in a cupboard except at weekends, though I soon overcame this minor problem by unscrewing the cupboard hinges. Sometimes when I was sent to my bedroom I would climb out of the window onto the balcony, then drop to the ground and be away to the woods, taking my chance of a hiding if I was found out.

SIBERIAN WINTER

The winter of 1947–8 was a real Siberian one, with snow and ice from Christmas to March and, to make matters worse, there was food and coal rationing. We had very little money and the house always seemed cold unless you were sitting on top of the fire. Lakes and ponds were frozen over, and even the tidal River Medway had ice along its margins. Almost everyone had burst pipes and we were no exception. Roads were blocked, but my mates and I made a great sledge using a curved piece of Anderson shelter. We would climb aboard at the top of Maple Hill and go down at great speed, never considering the danger.

A group of us lads went to the woods every day and collected wood chippings which we sold for a shilling a sack. We also went to Morgan's woodyard and pulled through the fencing any timber we could reach. Warmth was the most important thing to our families in that Siberian winter. One Saturday my mum told me to take my barrow to Rochester Gas Works to fetch a sack of coke. It cost ten shillings, which was a lot of money in those days. At the gas works I noticed that there was coke all over the ground where it was being unloaded from the barges, and thought, 'What a waste!' A few days later a friend and I rowed a small clinker-built dinghy from Strood pier across the river to the gas works. We tied up at the wall and clambered up the ladder. All around us there was coke, and we soon had a couple of sandbags full.

After that we found it easy to get coke. We made sure that Mrs Phillips, a pensioner who lived next door to me, and others like her, had plenty of coke and wood, and we also supplied coke to several women who had lost their husbands in the war. We were young Robin Hoods. Those who could afford to pay we charged five bob a sack, and then shared the money, spending it on fishing tackle and snares – even food, when we could get some.

Food rationing was a problem, but thankfully my uncles were keen on shooting and ferreting, and most weekends we crept into Lord Darnley's estate at Cobham woods in search of rabbits, pheasants and pigeons. We even ate swans. We rarely went without meat, and to this day one of my favourite dishes is rabbit pie, which few people know how to make. In exchange for rabbits the local butcher let me have whale meat and corned beef; when these were in short supply then he gave me a shilling for each rabbit.

Most days when I wasn't at school I went off into the woods or the chalk quarries, setting my snares and stalking rabbits with my Webley air-rifle. Sometimes I got grey squirrels, and at that time the council paid a bounty on the tails. At the council office we would send my friend's little sister in with just a couple of tails; if she reported that the lady was at the desk, we knew she would pay up without examining the tails, so we would cut the rest in half and double our money.

When, on his return from the Far East, one of my uncles learned that we had no meat because of rationing, he declared, 'I've been fighting the bloody Japanese for the past four years and I'm going to have meat for tomorrow's dinner!' We did – pheasants from Cobham woods. The keeper chased us, but we gave him the slip.

We spent so much time in the woods and quarries that we got to know the area really well. We always kept our eyes open for the gamekeeper, and once we were just a couple of yards away from his head, in an old oak tree as he sat below us having a smoke. He never could catch us.

PIGEONS FOR SALE

One way of earning some pennies was selling jackdaws to children who were too frightened to clamber down the quarry. A jackdaw was worth two shillings. I also sold pigeons at half a crown each, but getting them was more dangerous as I had to crawl under Rochester Bridge at night and grab them when they were roosting. The only time we could collect pigeons was on dark evenings; they always flew off if we tried to get them in the daylight. The operation took four of us, one at each end of the bridge, with Peter and I in the middle where there was a manhole cover. Once we got the 'all-clear' signal from the other two, Peter and I would lift the manhole cover and I would clamber down the ladder; then I would work my way along the narrow spans and girders, grabbing the roosting pigeons and stuffing them into a bag. Forty feet below were the swirling waters of the tidal River Medway.

When I had caught enough I would make my way back to the manhole and rap on the cover. When all was clear Peter would lift the cover and help me up. Then it was off home to put the pigeons in my shed for selling later to the juniors at school. I used to tell them that I had some very good homing pigeons for sale. 'You mustn't let them out for at least three months,' I told them, 'or they will fly away and not come back.'

I often wonder how many times we sold the same pigeons.

CHERRIES AND RED CHEEKS

One day I saw a big box of cherries outside Mr Mockett's, the greengrocer. 'Hey, look!' I said to my mates. 'Mockett's got some cherries. Let's get in single file and grab some.' I was at the back, and as I grabbed my cherries a hand lifted me off the ground.

'Gotcha, you little thief! Who's it going to be, me or your father?'

'You, Mr Mockett!'

'Get in the shop and bend over that sack of potatoes.'

Mockett picked up an orange box and pulled a piece from the bottom. The nails squealed in protest as he pulled the plank free. I gritted my teeth, and my mates watched through the window as Mockett whacked me with the plank.

'One, two, three! You won't steal anything from my shop again. Four, five – take that you little thief – six. That will teach you a lesson.'

Tears welled up in my eyes, but I didn't cry with my mates watching. My backside was stinging as I walked uncomfortably down the road with my friends. However, I was a hero because I hadn't cried.

All was not over. When I got home Mum shouted, 'It's tea time!'

'I don't want any tea,' I mumbled.

'You can still sit up at the table,' Mum said. I was sore and I couldn't keep still.

'Sit still on that chair,' Dad ordered. Then he said, 'Get upstairs to your bedroom.'

I went, and soon I heard his footsteps heavy on the stairs. He came into my bedroom and told me to pull down my trousers. I did.

'What have you been up to?' he asked.

'Scrumping cherries from Mr Mockett.'

'Oh, so you're a thief,' he yelled. 'A son of mine caught stealing!' He pulled off his belt. 'It's the buckle end for you, my lad,' he shouted.

The buckle lashed my backside and I cried out in pain.

'I'll teach you to be a thief.' Whack, whack, whack! 'Have you learned your lesson now?' He was still shouting.

'Yes,' I sobbed . . . 'Yes, yes!'

Even that wasn't the end of my troubles. At school next day in the gym I made out that I wasn't feeling well. Mr Ingham the teacher said, 'Get undressed, boy, and under that cold shower. Then you will feel all right.'

I undressed, and of course Ingham spotted the weals and bruises caused by my two hidings.

'What have you been punished for? And don't tell me any lies.'

'I got caught scrumping, sir.'

'A boy in my boxing team, a thief!' Ingham yelled. 'Don't ever do it again or you'll be thrown out of the team.'

Sheepishly I went off into the gym. It was a painful lesson, and I didn't get caught scrumping again.

FIRST ANGLING CLUB

In 1949 I joined my first angling club, the Maidstone Victory and Medway Preservation Society and, as my father worked at Winget's, I also joined their angling club. Winget's A C organized Sunday coach trips to their stretch of the River Beault at Hunton, and I remember one member, Albert, who never seemed to catch anything – we had to listen to him moaning all the way home about not having caught a sausage. On these coach trips, the senior members would go off to The Bull at lunchtime, Albert among them. On one October day he arrived back at his swim to find his float under the water and, thinking he had at last caught a fish, he struck with a flourish: out came two burnt sausages! We had tied them on his line for a laugh, and luckily he took it all in good part.

Another Winget's member, Bill Hall, had caught a 20lb pike on a little green frog – or so he used to tell us. Whenever Bill got on the coach we would all shout, 'any green frogs today, Bill?'. He had a lad, Bill junior, the same age as me, and we used to go fishing together. One day while Bill and I were cycling across Rochester Bridge, Bill's jacket burst into flames. We jumped off our bikes, and I took off my jacket and smothered the flames. Bill ended up with a badly burnt arm. We reckoned that someone must have thrown away a cigarette butt which somehow had landed in Bill's pocket. However, it didn't stop our fishing trips!

NIGHT ON THE RIVER

Soon I was spending every spare moment at the waterside. Several of my school friends fished as well, and during the school holidays we would often get the train from Strood station to Maidstone West and then change trains for Teston, Wateringbury or Yalding.

One day when I was fishing at Wateringbury, two anglers arrived in the late afternoon loaded down with tackle and lanterns. After they had settled down I went along to have a chat with them; I was always chatting with other anglers, hoping to learn different ways of fishing.

'Hello, have you caught anything?' I said.

'Just a couple of roach and a bream,' one of them said.

'Are you fishing all night?' I asked.

'Yes,' they told me.

'Can I fish with you, mister?'

'What will your mum say?' one asked.

'She won't mind. She lets me fish all the time,' I replied.

He wasn't altogether convinced and insisted that I should go home and ask my mother's permission. He must have thought I lived locally, because after I had wandered up the river to Wateringbury Station, bought some chews in the shop, and wandered back down the river, he believed me when I said that my mother had given me the okay. I was determined to fish all night.

For the next three hours I sat and watched these experts catch roach and bream on bread. When I asked how they kept the bread on the hook they said it was no problem because they were using bread flake. They helped me set up my tackle so that I could fish like they did, and even gave me some big quill floats for use when float legering. As it got dark so it got colder, and they had to watch their dough bobbins by the light of the lantern with a nightlight inside it. They were ever so kind to me. One of them wrapped me in his army overcoat so that I wouldn't get cold. They showed me how to put bread flake on the hook, and they let me bring in some of their roach and bream.

One of them said, 'Would you like me to take you home?'

'No,' I said firmly. 'I want to fish all night.' But after a while I fell asleep, and some time in the early hours I was shaken awake and a policeman was asking my name. It turned out that my parents had notified the police when I hadn't arrived home. The policeman collected up my tackle, and off home I went. I expected the hiding of my life, but all everyone wanted to know was whether I was all right. I was, of course; *and* I could now fish with bread flake, which my mates couldn't. Bread flake is still one of my favourite baits.

FISHING OUT OF SCHOOL

My schoolfriends and I spent many a day at the waterside when we should have been at school. We used to tell our parents that we were fishing in a match against another local school, and so we would be given our train fare and some sandwiches. Then instead of going to school, we would go off to the Medway. Peter Burstow, who was in my class, was a very keen angler, and he and I often went off to Cliffe marshes for the day when we should have been at school. We used to fish the Alpha Cement Works Angling Club water, which was private, but the water baliff never once caught us and the place was stuffed full of rudd. You could catch fish on just about any bait, and we had some huge eels with yellow bellies by legering worms. These eels fought harder than anything else we caught, and we had a dickens of a job unhooking them. It took two of us, and invariably we got covered in slime, sometimes losing our hook in the eel.

One day Peter and I caught over two hundred fish. We soon used up all our worms; and then we even ran out of flour and water paste, which we had learned to keep on the hook by mixing with sheep's wool collected from the fence posts. Undaunted, we used currants from our fruit cake, and we still caught fish – not very big, but we caught a lot. Finally we hunted around and found some pea bugs, and they tempted fish, too. The rudd in the Alpha Cement Works water would eat anything.

PIGS AND MINISTRY MEN

Looking back on the late forties I have to smile when I think of my uncles and their pig farms. They farmed at Walderslade near Chatham, and often at weekends I went to stay with Aunt Peg and Uncle Eddy. My uncle and I used to go round people's houses emptying the pig swill bins; those who kept a bin for us got a joint of pork every now and again for their trouble.

Farmers were not allowed to kill off their pigs just as they wished, and ministry men would come round to check on just how many pigs and piglets they had. It was the job of us children to hide them during these visits. We had a relative who worked in the Labour Exchange at Chatham and he used to tip us off, whereupon we had to go and get a pig and hide it away. One day I was detailed to haul an old boar off into the woods and hide there until the ministry men had gone. Now if you've never tried to move a pig against its will, then you have missed one of life's experiences: you drag it one pace forward, and then it drags you three paces backwards. I even tried to pull this one by its tail, but nothing seemed to work. Then a neighbour came across with a lump of wood with a nail in it, and thumped the nail into the pig's nose; I winced, and still do to this day, but the pig followed us to the woods. I complained that it was cruel, but was told it would be a lot worse for the boar if the ministry men found him. I guess it was rather like a bull having a ring through its nose.

Sometimes we would take a piglet home and hide it in the house. We couldn't always trust the neighbours, however, and sometimes they would report us to the authorities. But we were never caught, and we often had a big joint of pork despite the rationing.

SWAN FOR DINNER

By 1949 I was into wildfowling as well as fishing. My first shotgun was a Canadian single-barrel 12-bore. In the winter I would often go off before first light to shoot ducks on the marshes, and then come home for my tackle and spend the rest of the day fishing. One night I was on Cliffe marshes with an uncle. It was snowing hard and the wind was blowing gale force, and it was one of those nights when you question your sanity for being out at all. I was crouched in a mud hole trying my hardest to spot a duck in the swirling snow, when three geese came flying low against the wind. I crouched down: would this be my lucky day? Would I get my first goose? They continued to come in, and then I was up swinging the gun. I pulled the trigger on the leading bird, felt the thump from the gun on my shoulder, and watched the goose stagger and glide off to crash on the marsh some distance away.

The dog was sent for the retrieve, and we were shocked to find my goose was actually a swan. But with meat rationing there was no way I was going to leave that swan, and it ended up in the oven. It wasn't the first: I remember eating swan at the end of the war to celebrate VE day. Many swans must have ended up that way during the 1940s.

GANG FIGHTS AND MISCHIEF

Of course I didn't always fish when I was out of school. We had a gang, the Temple Boys, named after the Knights Templar, and as well as having bows and arrows – the arrows tipped with copper fuse-wire – we also had catapults, air pistols and air-rifles. I never went anywhere without my catapult and a few ball bearings.

My mother didn't like guns, so my shotgun was left at my Aunt Peg's house in Luton. Aunt Peg let me do anything. When there was a world boxing championship on the radio in the early hours of the morning, I would go off to Aunt Peg's to listen to it with my uncle. I spent quite a bit of time at Aunt Peg and Uncle Eddy's, roaming the fields and woods with my mates. We had loads of fun together, and I had lots of girlfriends in Luton. On Saturday afternoons we sometimes went down to Chatham High Street with a few mice in our pockets. We used to drop them onto the floor in Woolworth's and then say, quite casually, to the shoppers, 'Look, there's a mouse!' and there would be pandemonium, with women screaming and running; then we used to walk quietly away with a sweet and innocent look on our faces.

In my pigeon shed at home I had dug out the earth from under the floorboards and made a wooden box to hold my air-rifle and pistol and my collection of sheath-knives, and anything else I didn't want Mum to know about.

We lived at Willow Road, and not far away was Darnley Road where there were a lot of rough boys – the Darnley Roadites, we called them. If they caught you in the woods on your own then you were in trouble because they would strip off all your clothes and throw you in the stinging nettles. They did this to me once, but only once: I made sure I was never caught again. In Darnley Road lived the Summers, the Barnards, the Whites, the Scales and others, all large families and all in one big gang, and we had many fights with them, sometimes coming home with torn clothes, bloody noses and bruised and battered faces. But we gave as good as we got, fighting with fists, feet and staves and never giving an inch. Sometimes when a gang from Rochester came over the bridge we would join up with the Darnley Roadites, and then all hell would be let loose, with catapults, bows and arrows, bits of piping, staves and anything else we could lay our hands on. They were really bloody affairs with battered shins, black eyes, broken teeth, bleeding gums, even a few tear-stained eyes.

In summer we often got in to Rochester swimming baths by climbing over the fence. Another method was to take off one of the fence panels, then we would all creep through and replace the panel. We never got caught, although to this day I don't know how we got away with it.

Strood pier was a popular gathering place whenever there were ships in from Sweden, Norway or Finland. They came laden with wood pulp, and when their crews had been to the pubs we would row them back to the ships and earn money for cigarettes and other luxuries, like girlfriends! In summer a paddle steamer used to be tied up at the pier, and to show off to the girls we would go hand-over-hand up the mooring ropes and climb on board. And when one of the crew members came to chase us away we use to run round the deck until we had had enough and then dive over the side and swim back to the pier.

In the winter we would all go to the Wardona cinema in Strood High Street. It was known as 'the bug hutch', and we had several ways of getting in without paying, though usually one of us paid to get in and then went into the toilet and opened the window for the rest to climb through.

Beer and lemonade bottles were worth money, and many a time we nipped over the fence at one pub to grab a crate of beer bottles and take them back to another pub that stocked the same brands. Then we could buy fags, usually Turf or Woodbines. One day the Temple Boys got together with the Darnley Roadites and went to a quarry on the Cuxton Road; there, with catapults, bows and arrows and rocks we stopped the workmen from going home for two hours. Whenever they came out of their hut we fired a shower of ball bearings, arrows and rocks, and they had to run back into the shed. As thirteen- and fourteen-year-olds it was good fun, until the local gamekeeper caught Dennis, one of our gang. We gathered round the keeper, our catapults loaded, and told him that if he didn't let our mate go we would fire ball bearings at him. It did the trick, and he let Dennis go with a warning about what would happen if he ever caught us there again. We ran like hell, but I don't know what would have happened if he hadn't let Dennis go.

Another of our tricks was to collect slow-worms and then creep up and throw them on a courting couple. There would be a scream and the bloke would come chasing after us, but we could run like whippets and we were never caught.

Most boys collected birds' eggs, and I was no different; I had a very good collection laid out neatly in boxes filled with sawdust. When I found the nest of a bird whose egg I didn't have, I used to count the eggs: if there were four or more then I would take just one, first checking it wasn't addled. Also in my bedroom I had a big wooden box with a glass top where I used to keep grass snakes, lizards, slow-worms and, sometimes, frogs. And then one time when I was away at an army camp with the cadets they all got away. I never found out where they went or what happened to them.

PLAYING AT SOLDIERS

I joined the navy cadets as soon as I was old enough; my father having been in the navy before he was killed meant that I was eligible to join. I had a happy twelve months learning to tie knots, going out rowing and sailing, and learning to march properly. I was also able to do some boxing. Then when I was old enough, I joined the Royal Engineers' Cadet Force and I really enjoyed my time with them, going on many camps, and shooting with .303 rifles and Sten guns. Later on I learnt to shoot a Bren gun, and how to strip the guns down quickly. This was the life for me. On weekend camps we went on manoeuvres, we had sports days when I could take part in the boxing and the athletics, and we went away for a two-week camp with the regular army.

One evening we were supposed to go to a boxing match at the Royal Naval Barracks, but we didn't go because there was a terrible diaster at Chatham: a bus driver mowed down a group of marching Royal Marine cadets as they headed for the boxing tournament. Many young cadets died on that terrible night: it was one of the worst ever accidents on our roads. My parents were listening to the nine o'clock news on the wireless when they heard about the accident, but all they knew was that a number of cadets had been killed in Military Road, Chatham. They thought that I had gone there, so when I arrived home they were greatly relieved.

One year we went away for two weeks to Landguard Camp at Felixstowe. One of the cooks was a Sergeant Maplesden who had worked with my father at Winget's, and I remember he once made me a huge bread pudding which I shared with my mates: we were always hungry in those days. Our CO was Lt.-Col. Higgins, who had also worked at Winget's, and he often asked me how I was. It was during that camp that he presented me with my first stripe. I enjoyed every minute of my three years in the cadets, especially when we were away at camp or on manoeuvres; but, as fishing and girls began taking up more of my time, I decided to leave.

Something I really enjoyed was going to Rochester library to browse among the fishing and shooting books. I was an avid reader and had joined the library in Strood when I was seven years old. Reading was about the only thing I could do properly; it transported me to different parts of the world and different times in history, and I was never bored.

Then I came across, in my view, the best angling writer of all time, Hugh Tempest Sheringham. I became friends with HTS, as well as with J.H.R. Bazley, Trent Otter, BB – who was, of course, Dennis Watkins-Pitchford – Bernard Venables (and Mr Crabtree), Faddist, Skues, Halford and many more. My bible was the Lonsdale Library book *Fine Angling for Coarse Fish*; I still have it to this day. Yes, the library was the golden gateway to a wealth of knowledge about angling, shooting and natural history.

Hugh Sheringham wrote the book *Anglers' Hours*, and in its first chapter, 'At Dawn of Day', he captures the whole feeling of angling. It was through his writing that I came to love the River Kennet, which I think is England's most beautiful river. In the course of writing this book I had a day on the Kennet with my friend Mark Williams; as we sat there in the warm summer sunshine, legering a piece of bread crust, I felt that we had almost become a part of that lovely river. As we sat a kingfisher darted up and down; we could smell the water mint and the cow parsley; we heard the drone of insects and saw the flying display of the emperor dragonfly. The river bubbled and gurgled as the current hit the far bank and then swung across to my bank; the force of this water would push the bait under the willow branches downstream of my swim. At the end of the day the sun disappeared in the west and the sky turned shades of pink, blue, red and orange. A blackbird serenaded us from the top of a riverside willow. It was the perfect end to a summer's day. No other river can give me such contentment, although many do come close.

We fished with cane rods and old reels, the same type of tackle I used on my first visit to the Kennet way back in 1948, and we caught two barbel on crust bait. They weighed 6lb 4oz and 7lb 7oz, the latter a personal best Kennet barbel for me. I also caught an American signal crayfish, an imported species which I had never seen before. This alien is killing off the British crayfish, so it is one we could do without.

The Kennet has never let me down. I have enjoyed every minute of my time on the banks of this, the nicest of rivers.

KENNET: TWO POUND ROACH

It was Sheringham's writing about the Kennet that caused me to spend thirty-seven years, on and off, trying to catch a two pound Kennet roach. In 1985 I achieved my dream with a fish of 2lb ½oz.

I was with Len Head. We had travelled from his Essex home one Saturday morning and bought our day tickets from the Old Mill at Aldermaston. We wandered downriver, and as we crossed the old wooden bridge I glanced over the reeds.

'Blimey, Len, just take a look at these big roach,' I said. We saw a shoal of seven roach, all over the pound mark.

'You take this swim, Len,' I said, 'and I'll move into the next one. There's a good chance of catching all of those fish.'

'No mate,' Len told me. 'I want to fish for barbel.'

Further downriver I put Len in one of the favoured barbel swims. 'See you later mate,' I said. 'I'm going after those roach.'

I went back upstream to the roach swim and sat down, wondering how to get a bait to the fish. Then I noticed a lot of fry in the margins, and dropped a handful of gentles in for them. As the gentles sank, the current took hold of them and they went off downstream across the gravel patch where the roach were feeding. How lucky can an angler be! I dropped some more gentles into the margins and, sure enough, these also drifted into the roach shoal. That was enough. I tackled up with my 11-foot light Avon rod, a centre-pin reel and some 2lb breaking strain line. A swan shot link leger and a size 16 hook direct to the line completed the tackle. Baiting with two gentles I made an underhand cast, and watched as the bait settled on the gravel patch. Within minutes I struck and was into a nice roach which weighed around the one-and-a-half pound mark.

I walked upstream and carefully released the fish where it wouldn't disturb the rest of the shoal. Then it was back to the roach swim where, in three casts, I had three more pound-plus roach. Each time I caught a fish I repeated the process of taking it upstream before releasing it.

There were three fish left in the shoal as, once again, I baited with two gentles and cast out so that the bait settled on the gravel patch. Once more the rod tip was gently pulled round, and soon another fish was in the landing net. It looked bigger than the other fish: could it go to two pounds?

I went down to Len's swim and asked him to weight the roach for me. I couldn't bear to watch, but then heard Len say, 'Two pounds and half an ounce, mate!'

At long last I'd done it, a two-pounder from the Kennet! I took some pictures and then it was back to the swim 'and another roach. Six out of seven! The last roach glided away out of sight. I've had dozens of two-pound roach from lots of different waters, but that was the one I wanted most. My dream of catching one of Sheringham's pigeon-chested roach had finally come true.

Today I have over 1,600 books at home, including all those by Hugh Tempest Sheringham, and that love for books started at the age of seven when I was at the junior school. And it was all thanks to my teacher at primary school who taught me to read.

CARP FEVER

One day when Peter Burstow and I were fishing Leybourne Lake we were told about a lake at Snodland that held big carp; also that the fishing belonged to Gravesend Kingfishers Angling and Preservation Society, a club that had some waters on Cliffe marshes. I decided to cycle out there and look at the lakes, and I soon found them. The two lakes, separated by a dirt road that runs across the marshes to the coastguard houses, were not far from the Alpha cement works. It was a place that Charles Dickens had written about in *Great Expectations*, and on a black night it was a creepy place to be on your own.

An angler was fishing what I learned was Windmill Lake, and I watched as he caught several big rudd. My appetite was whetted and I decided to try and join the club. I chatted with the club member and obtained the address of the secretary, and that evening sat down and wrote a letter, in my best hand-writing, asking if I could join. I received an application form which I filled in and sent off with a postal order for five shillings. A few days later, equipped with my new membership card, I was on my bike to Paddlesworth Lake, a flooded claypit owned by the local cement works and leased to the club. This pit contained carp, rudd – thousands of them, but which all seemed stunted – some roach and a few perch. It was the carp that interested me, and in fact they became an obsession; I just had to catch one of these magnificent fish.

Two-thirds of the bankside of this three-acre pit was covered in trees and bushes. At the roadside end of the lake the banks were steep, and being of clay, treacherous when wet; one false slip and you were in ten feet of water from which it was difficult to get out again. At the opposite end there was a large reedbed and a small island – in fact the island was home to millions of biting red ants. Black ants I have never found to be a problem, but every time I waded out to that island I was bitten to pieces.

The bottom of the pit was littered with all manner of rubbish, including rusty cable which was a real trap for tackle but a favourite place for fish to swim around when hooked. There was also an old truck, and that was ideal for busting tackle on. There were fallen trees and masses of Canadian pond-weed, but the one good thing about the water was that it was sheltered from the wind most of the time.

31

Two types of anglers fished the pit in the late 1940s: those who wanted to catch anything, which meant mostly stunted rudd or, if they were lucky, a carp of four or five pounds which was considered a good fish but hard to catch; and then there was the dedicated carp angler who fished for nothing but carp throughout the summer months. The carp angler fished in three ways. The first method was to use a float with gentles, worms or a paste bait flavoured with honey. The second approach was using unweighted floatless tackle with just a large hook tied on the end of the line and baited with plain white bread paste, usually the size of a bantam's egg but even as big as a chicken's egg on occasion. Our special bait of the day was brown bread and honey paste, but that was only if Granny would give me some honey. Mum wouldn't often let me have honey, though sometimes I managed to take a bit when no one was looking. There was trouble if she found out, though.

The third method was the use of a matchbox-sized piece of crust, fished on the surface. And very exciting it was, too, to see a carp of five pounds come up from the depths towards the bait and circle it for up to thirty minutes, often nudging it with its lips and then leaving it alone.

The pit had a carp of about ten pounds, which to us youngsters was huge. It consumed many of my waking hours, and probably all of my sleeping ones. This big common carp would roll on the crust bait, hitting it with its tail, and as the bread drifted away on the surface the fish would feed safely on the small pieces.

Early in 1949 I had been given a tank aerial about fourteen feet long. My Uncle Eddy helped me to make it into a fishing rod, but a success it was not. So, after a rethink, the aerial was cut down to nine feet and made a nice spinning rod which caused the downfall of several pike. The reel was an old walnut star-back reel 3½in. in diameter; it was fitted with a check, and came with some antique line, very thick and of dubious breaking strain. Attached to the end of the line was a length of thick catgut to which I could tie a hook. It had been used for pike fishing all through the previous winter.

FIRST CARP

From the start of the season I had been going to Paddlesworth pit at every opportunity, either fishing, watching the carp, or talking to other anglers. Most of the time I fished I could see that the carp were coming close to my bait, but I just couldn't get one to pick it up. It was exasperating, to say the least, and I used to get very angry because I couldn't catch one . . . that was until late July.

It was a Friday, and I had cycled to Paddlesworth pit with Peter Tillitt. Our idea was to camp for a few days so that we could fish day and night, and we chose as our pitch the top of a high bank on the western side of the lake. The tent was a small white one known as a pup tent, and there was just enough room inside for the two of us. Our cooking stove was an old paraffin primus, and for light we had a hurricane lamp. We had no sleeping bags or camp beds, just a couple of old army blankets and some big safety pins.

We arrived in the rain, pitched the tent and wrapped ourselves in our old gas capes to keep dry. Soon the sky cleared, the sun came out and it turned very warm. We watched an angler on the other side of the pit catch a carp. I was envious and wished that I could catch such a fish. Then, looking down from the high bank where the tent was pitched, I spotted a mirror carp of about five pounds. I grabbed my rod bag and tackled up. It was with fumbling fingers and a fast-beating heart that I threaded the line through the rings and tied on a hook, all the time frightened that the carp would swim off.

I baited with a piece of brown bread and honey paste, pulled a few feet of line from the reel, and dropped the bait into the margin about twelve inches away from the nose of the fish, which was still rooting about in the bottom. There was no reaction from the carp, which continued to dig into the mud causing the water to colour up. Only the occasional bubble appeared on the surface, something that Richard Walker in his *Stillwater Angling* called smoke-screening.

Through the murky water I watched as the fish straightened up onto an even keel and moved towards the bait. My heart thumped, my mouth was dry and my hands were shaking as I willed the fish to pick up my bait. Then it tilted its head downwards and the bait disappeared. With no more thought I struck upwards, there was a boil in the water and the fish shot out into the lake, my old wooden reel screaming, the line disappearing off its spool. Then everything stopped: the fish had buried itself in the weed.

Peter suggested trying to pull the line in a seesaw motion. I did, but nothing happened. Then one of the senior members came round from the other side of the pit; he also told me to try pulling the line in a seesaw movement. I tried again and the fish started to move, taking more line off the reel. The older angler said, 'Lay the rod over to the left, lad.' I did so and the fish turned, and I started to take in some line. But how was I going to get the fish out of the water without a landing net? This problem was soon solved when the older angler told Peter to go round and get his net. I don't think Peter had ever run so fast in his life – he was back in no time and, with the fish wallowing on the surface, the older angler took the net and scooped out my first carp. I was a happy boy. The fish was put on the club scales, and it weighed 4½lb exactly. I left Peter and cycled off home to tell Mum the good news, then cycled all the way back to continue our carp fishing. Forty years on, I'm still fishing for carp.

One attractive place I fished was known as Laughing Waters. There were two lakes alongside the London A2 near Cobham in Kent. The larger lake of some six acres was gin clear with lots of weed, and it held a good head of perch, roach and rudd plus a few good pike; we often wondered if it could produce a twenty-pounder. The smaller lake of less than two acres had rhododendron bushes around its banks, and it contained lots of common carp which could be caught on floating crust. Sometimes we would catch up to eight in a night session.

We were forbidden to visit the place because, our parents told us, men from London did naughty things there with ladies in the backs of their cars. But of course we still went there because it was only a short bike ride from home and the fish were fairly easy to catch. My best fish was a perch of 1½lb, and my best carp weighed 7lb. What was also good about the place was that just down the road the farmer grew strawberries, and in June and early July we could feast on strawberries *and* catch carp.

I fished for the carp with floating bread crust, using 10lb Luron line and a size 6 Allcock's Model Perfect hook. I used to grease the line to make it float, and cast out the bread so that it drifted under the rhododendron bushes. Then I would pull off some more line from the reel and fold a piece of silver paper from a Players cigarette packet over the line as a bite indicator.

My friends and I would sit quietly watching the waterbirds, and sometimes a carp would appear near the bait and we would sit there, mouths dry, eyes bolting out, willing the fish to take our crust. Sometimes the fish would cruise around the bait for twenty minutes or more, but as soon as the crust disappeared in a swirl we would be on our feet striking hard over our shoulder. The rod would be pulled down towards the water as the fish fought hard to get in among the tree roots. We never gave much line: it was like a tug-of-war when sometimes we won and at other times it was the fish.

On the A2 just outside Laughing Waters there was a mobile coffee stall, and during our night fishing sessions we would go there to buy hot pies and coffee. It was all good fun, and some evenings we would have these good-looking women walking round the lake in the evening after dinner at the lakeside restaurant. You can imagine what thoughts we seventeen- and eighteen-year-olds had! In fact I had a romance for a few weeks with one of the waitresses. She would bring me tea and sandwiches to the waterside, and if the carp weren't feeding then it would be cuddles in the back of the restaurant. Those were good days!

ANGLING BY COACH

Amongst the most enjoyable events in the forties and fifties were the angling club coach trips with the Kingfishers or Winget's angling clubs to various venues. The coach used to pick up my friends and me outside St Nicholas'

Church in Strood. As juniors we had to sit in the front of the coach, the back being reserved for senior members. One venue we fished was Grove Ferry on the Kentish Stour; it was full of fish and they were easy to catch most days. The river was tidal, and I liked it particularly when it was high tide around noon so that we could fish both the flood and the ebb tide. The top bait was either bread crust or bread flake, although a bunch of gentles would often work, but had the disadvantage of attracting eels.

There was a pub at Grove Ferry, and there the senior members went at lunchtime. To get from one side of the river to the other you had to use a ferry (these days there is a bridge in place of the ferry).

Pound roach were commonplace in the late forties and early fifties, and Grove Ferry was the ideal place to fish with a Thames roach pole using crust flake or paste as bait. To watch some of the old London anglers sitting on their black boxes or baskets and fishing with their 18-foot bamboo poles with hollowed-out mahogany butt joints was a great pleasure. They were masters at playing big fish on the pole, unshipping the joints as they brought the fish to the net, gleaming pound roach and three-pound bream.

My tackle was a 16-foot rod with a whole cane butt joint and split bamboo middle and top joints. Rods like that were not available from ordinary tackle shops; they were only made by Mr Clarkson of Rochester, who built some lovely rods. I never used my fixed spool reel for float fishing, preferring a centre-pin reel – usually an Aerial, a Rapidex or a Speedia – with 3lb breaking strain line. My floats were always cork on quill that would take 5 or 6 BB shot, and my hooks ranged from nos. 12 to 6 depending on the bait.

We used either bread flake, or cube, or paste which had to be prepared the night before. To make bread cube we would take the crust and some crumb from a two-day old loaf and lay it on a wooden board covered with a damp cloth; then another damp cloth and a board were placed on top, and the whole lot was compressed using a heavy weight, usually a couple of flat irons borrowed from my mother. In the morning I would cut the bread into cubes and put these into an Oxo tin. Using the white crumb from some stale bread, I made up my bread paste and flavoured it with custard powder or aniseed.

Bread paste has always been a good bait for me, and I still use it to this day. It will tempt roach, bream, chub and rudd, and if you add some cheese it's a particularly good bait when fishing in coloured water for roach, chub and barbel. Bunches of gentles were also used, despite the eel problem, but I reckon they are the most overrated of baits. I very rarely use gentles today, and I think that if more people used bread or worms they would catch better fish.

We used to have a shilling sweepstake for the best fish and a shilling for the top weight. On the way home we always stopped at a pub, but we juniors had to sit outside the pub or on the coach with a glass of lemonade and some crisps. However, as soon as we became senior members we were allowed at the back of the coach with all the tobacco smoke, the card schools, smutty jokes and the *News of the World*.

With the growth of car ownership the coach trips disappeared: it was the end of an era. I would dearly like to see the return of angling coach trips. They created a friendship among all the anglers, and the winner would more often than not tell all and sundry how he had won the match or caught the biggest fish. We need to help the environment, and resurrecting the coach trips would be a super way of doing so. A forty-seater coach would reduce by at least twenty the number of cars out on the roads at weekends, and besides, anglers would perhaps once again enjoy the comradeship of those days.

CHAPTER 3

Heroes and Helpers

Mr Crabtree

When I first held rod and line,
Mr Crabtree was my guide;
His teaching and his sense of fun,
The knowledge that I drew upon.
The pages seemed to come alive,
His love that was the countryside.
A hero to so many boys,
He painted wisdom, offered joy.
And now I've realized a dream
And met the man who gave to me
This firm foundation in my life.
To shake his hand filled me with pride;
Bernard has become a friend,
To share the love and to defend
The beauty that is God's alone,
The beauty that is Nature's home.

Lorraine Davies

Throughout my life I have been very fortunate to have met some great men. Not all were household names, but they were all people who cared. Some were military men, others naturalists, wildfowlers and anglers, and also men who devoted their time and energy to helping those less fortunate in our society. Five of these became my personal heroes.

A CHAT AT CHARTWELL

Sir Winston Churchill, our wartime leader, had a stirring voice which roused the nation in its hour of need, and even listening to those speeches again today makes me feel proud to be an Englishman. I met the great man one September

37

day in 1952 at his Chartwell home near Westerham. I had gone out on my bike, looking for new places to fish. I had heard there was a lake somewhere in the area, and as I passed the gates of Chartwell I decided, on impulse, to go in and see what it was like. No-one stopped me as I pushed my bike up the drive. Close to the house I came across Sir Winston himself, standing by the house, and I could see his painting easel nearby. He was just as I had imagined him to be.

'I'm sorry, sir,' I said 'I seem to have got lost. I was looking for a carp lake.'

I was just turning to go when the great man said, 'That's all right, young man. Can I help you?'

I explained that I had come from Rochester and that I was a keen angler. I told him about our house being bombed by doodlebugs, and thanked him for what he had done for us during the war. I was a very nervous sixteen-year-old, but he soon put me at my ease and I must have spent at least twenty minutes there, during which time he talked about art and I talked about fishing. He even invited me to have a cup of tea, which was brought out to us.

I was in London in 1965 the day the nation saluted its great wartime leader on his way to his final resting place in Oxfordshire, and I'm not ashamed to admit that my eyes were filled with tears.

CHIEF OF THE CHINDITS

Another hero of my boyhood days was General Orde Wingate, leader of the Chindits. The Chindits were a part of SEAC (South East Asia Command) which worked behind the Japanese lines, notably in Burma, during the Second World War. They attacked troop trains and supply lines, blew up ammunition dumps and created havoc wherever they found the enemy.

Orde Wingate died in the jungles of Burma while fighting the Japanese, who were responsible for the death of my parents. It is impossible to forget all the suffering and death the Japs caused. Sadly I never met Orde Wingate, but since I had two relatives who served in the Chindits I made it my business to get to know a lot about this great warrior. He must have been some man.

STIRLING SERVICE

Then there was Sir David Stirling who initiated the Long-Range Desert Group in the Middle East during the Second World War, formed to attack the German positions from the rear. On one of these raids Stirling was captured and put into a prisoner-of-war camp, from which he escaped. He was again captured, and this time sent to Colditz Castle near the town of Leipzig where he continued to cause trouble for the Germans. The group was resurrected in 1947 during the Malayan Campaign against the Communist terrorists, and it then became the Special Air Service.

What wonderful service the SAS has given us, looking after British interests throughout the world! There was the time in 1984 when they stormed the Iranian Embassy in London and captured the terrorists holding it at gunpoint; and before we invaded the Falkland Islands in 1982 the SAS was there, blowing up ammunition dumps and aircraft. Along with the Special Boat Service they lost twenty-two men in a tragic helicopter accident in the South Atlantic during that war. Then again they were on the ground in Iraq during the Gulf war, giving immense service to the ground and air personnel.

I have not only had the good fortune to meet David Stirling, I have also met his brother Col. Bill Stirling of the SAS; this was when visiting the Kier estate in Scotland, with Scottish gundog champion Ron Montgomery, to take part in a pheasant-shooting day. And I met one of the 'Avengers' girls, the lovely Diana Rigg, who is married to Bill's son Archie Stirling; I took some photographs of her with a black labrador named Bonnie, bred and trained by Ron Montgomery at his Scottish kennels.

THE CRABTREE CONNECTION

My other two heroes are anglers. One is a very special artist, namely Bernard Venables who created Mr Crabtree. The Crabtree influence came to me through a comic strip in the *Daily Mirror*. Every time I got hold of the paper I used to read about Garth, Karen, Dawn and the professor; then it was Jane; and finally Mr Crabtree, the angler who was always catching big fish. I was enthralled by Venables' writing and drawings on perch fishing.

In my last year at Temple School I decided that I would have to work hard if I was to get a good report, and in doing so I won the school Book Prize. The school secretary told me to choose a book to the value of one guinea, and I opted for *Mr Crabtree Goes Fishing* by Bernard Venables; this title sold two million copies. The secretary came to me a few days later and said, 'The book you have chosen is only five shillings, and you can have one for one guinea.'

'I know Miss, but that's the one I want. Could I have some floats with the rest of the money?'

'You can't do that. It's one book only,' she replied.

'Then it's got to be *Mr Crabtree*,' I said.

The character Mr Crabtree showed us how to enjoy being by the waterside, and in a wonderful way he showed us what fishing was all about. When I read about the Royalty fishery on the River Avon, I thought it was where King George VI fished! I was an avid reader of Bernard Venables and collected all his books; moreover it was Bernard who made *Creel* such a wonderful magazine, and when he left the editor's chair it immediately went downhill and became just an ordinary magazine.

On my fifty-second birthday I had the best present I could have wished for: I travelled down to Bernard's home to record a series of programmes for BBC Radio 5 and Radio Lancashire. He was so kind, and his wife Eileen made me a wonderful lunch. I took all my copies of his books, every one of which he signed, and we chatted about angling and about the better things from the past. Since that first visit Bernard, Eileen, my wife Kate and I often get together over a meal and a bottle of wine. The conversation is always sparkling and full of interest, and it's a real treat to be with them. Recently at one of these get-togethers the subject turned (as it usually does) to the old days when we both lived in Kent, but on this occasion we went further back in time, back to the days before I was born, when Bernard lived on Romney Marsh. He told us a story about the Romney Marsh sheep fairs when he was just six years old and his mother dressed him up as a bluebell fairy. I can just imagine him!

Bernard is first and foremost an artist, and I know no-one who can capture the countryside, its wildlife and fish in quite the way he does. His paintings, whether in oils or in water colours, are to my mind the best, and for me he captures the true spirit of angling. In 1949 his wonderful book *A Fisherman's Testament* was published by A & C Black. There is a chapter simply entitled 'Pike', and in it he writes about his good friend St John Cooper catching a 30¼lb pike from a Berkshire lake; last summer Bernard and I visited that same water to fish for tench in true Crabtree style with bamboo rods and centre-pin reels.

Bernard enjoys being at the waterside as much today as he did all those years ago when he was fishing on Romney Marsh as a boy. Thank you, Bernard, for Mr Crabtree and for all the other books which have flowed from your pen and for the pictures from your brush.

WALKER, MY GURU

Richard Walker is my fifth and final hero, and he showed us that we could catch big fish by design and not just by luck. In 1953 his *Stillwater Angling* was published, and what a book that was! I had ordered my copy from W.H. Smith in Chatham weeks before publication date, and had been told when the books would be on sale. On the appointed day, I was outside the shop at 8.30 a.m. waiting for it to open; at nine o'clock the doors were unlocked and within two minutes I had my book. I stood there, spellbound, flicking through the pages.

This was it! No Royal Dockyard College for me that day; I went off home. I wasn't interested in physics, maths, English or chemistry, and our ex-Royal Naval officer teachers wouldn't understand *Stillwater Angling*. When I arrived back home, Mum asked, 'What are you doing here?'

I just said, 'I'm going to read *Stillwater Angling* by Richard Walker,' and went off to my bedroom to read the book from cover to cover. Then I started it all over again and found it hard to put down even though I wanted to go to the waterside and start to fish as Richard was telling us. In his introduction on catching big fish he writes of the five essentials, and truly, if we all took his advice we *would* catch big fish. This book should be read by anglers everywhere, because the rules are as true today as they were in 1953, and should be followed to the letter.

I first met Richard Walker in the fifties at a show in London. Many other anglers were queuing to meet the great man as, with autograph book in hand, I asked for his signature. I addressed him as 'Sir,' but: 'Call me Dick,' he said charmingly.

'Yes sir,' I replied. He told me about his carp fishing and gave me advice about catching carp from my local waters. A few days later I sent him a letter with some questions about catching chub from the River Beault, and received a wonderful letter back in beautiful copperplate handwriting answering all my questions. I was also a great fan of 'Walker's Pitch' in the *Angling Times* every week: he made me realise that I, too, could catch the big ones, and my angling improved in leaps and bounds.

One day in January I was on the River Medway with the water bank high. It was cold, wet and windy, and I was fishing with a piece of crust in the margins when another angler appeared. 'Caught anything?' he asked.

'No, not yet,' I answered.

My new acquaintance then said, 'I'd like to see what that bloody Walker would catch in these conditions.' With that my rod tip pulled round, I struck and soon had a nice roach of around a pound and a half in the net.

I turned and said, 'That's what Richard Walker would catch if he was fishing here today.' He stalked off up the river muttering under his breath. I was always getting into arguments with older anglers over Walker and his writing; they would say such things as, 'I'd like to see him catch fish from this lake,' or 'Let's see him catch fish from here with his rope and his shark hooks,' as they fished with tiny hooks baited with gentles and still couldn't catch a fish. But my friends and I usually fished as Walker had suggested.

As a true Walker disciple I was kitted out with a battered Trilby hat, Mk IV carp and Avon rods, laminated cane-armed landing net, Felton cross-wind and Mitchell 300 reels, water thermometer and Heron bite indicators. Even today I'm still using this tackle . . . and I still have a Trilby hat. Sometime in the fifties there was a centre-page spread of my hero fishing for tench on a Lincolnshire lake. He was wearing a crewneck jumper, and I showed it to my mother and asked her if she could knit me one like it. She agreed, on condition that I got the wool, and a week later I had that jumper.

I collected his books, had them signed, and read all his material in the coarse and game fishing magazines. I even started to fly fish the big Midland reservoirs the way he suggested. I admired and loved the man like a father; in fact he really was the father of modern angling, and he gave us so much. One saying of his that I will never forget is 'A fish will eat anything unless taught not to'.

In the mid-fifties Richard was writing regularly for the *London Evening Standard*, and he asked me to write his column one week on bream fishing in the South East. I did, and a copy of that column stayed in my wallet until it faded away. Today I treasure the precious moments I spent with Richard and his wife Pat. Time and again I sit and listen to the recordings I made with the great man, and when I am at the waterside trying to catch a fish I often say quietly to myself, 'How would you do it, Richard?'; and sometimes when I catch a good fish I feel certain that he guided my movements. It was through Richard Walker that I became a more caring and better person, and that was because *he* cared.

With his death in 1985, angling lost one of its champions; but he was our guru, our spiritual leader, and his influence lives on. Soon after his death his widow, Pat Marston-Walker, organized a memorial service at Biggleswade church and I travelled down from Lancashire to record the event, which was a very moving one. People from all walks of life came to pay their last respects to the man who had given them so much. I then dashed back home so that some of the material could be broadcast on BBC Radio Lancashire the next day.

With the permission of BBC Radio Lancashire, producer-presenter Simon Johnson and I also put together a cassette tape entitled *The Best of Hook Line and Sinker*, as a tribute to Richard Walker. The tape contained interviews from my BBC radio programmes, and all the proceeds went to charity.

One of the greatest honours for me was to host a chat show at the Queensway hall, Dunstable, in May 1988. It had been organized in memory of Richard Walker by Mike Kavanagh, conference organizer for the Carp Society, and commemorated fifty years of carp fishing. Before the event I visited three famous anglers who would not be able to attend, in order to record their memories of the great man. Together with one of angling's nice guys, Len Head of Sudbury, we went to Dick Kefford in Suffolk, Dennis Watkins-Pitchford – known to millions as BB – at his home in Northamptonshire, and then to Lincolnshire to interview Maurice Ingham. And it is time I put the record straight for all those who accused me of making money from this event: let me assure you that I gave my time and work freely, out of love for Richard

Walker. I did not even want my expenses paid, and I made this clear to the conference organizer when we discussed the project. Further, to the best of my knowledge no one else was paid for contributing either; indeed, I purchased out of my own pocket two tankards which I had engraved, to present to Mike and Len. We worked as a team, and it was a successful event.

The invitation to host the conference arrived on my fiftieth birthday in October 1987, and if I had been offered the choice between a knighthood or to host the Richard Walker memorial chat show, the latter would have won hands down. After the show Pat Marston-Walker said how much she had enjoyed the day, and for me that was reward enough.

Since 1987 I have been trying to get Richard Walker honoured in Westminster Abbey for his contributions to angling and rabbit breeding; his book *The Flemish Giant Rabbit*, published in 1946, is still the bible of rabbit breeders today. Then there is his war record: he gave honourable service at the Royal Aircraft Establishment in Farnborough. And finally, though not least, he was a gentleman to anglers everywhere and a great ambassador for all true sportsmen. I have written thousands of words about the great man in letters to Her Majesty the Queen, to Prince Charles, to the Prime Minister (at the time Margaret Thatcher), to the Dean of Westminster, to dozens of MPs and to the 'Letters' pages of newspapers. I will continue to fight so that Richard Walker is honoured by the nation. Many of us cannot understand why he was never given recognition in the honours list during his lifetime, when such awards were made to pop stars and to other sportspeople.

HELPERS

When I was eleven Mr Roberts and Mr Carrol, two anglers who worked with my father at Winget's Engineering, often took me fishing. I learnt a lot from them, in particular how to use hempseed as both groundbait and hookbait. Their favourite fishing spot was at Wateringbury on the River Medway. A few yards above the bridge was an outlet pipe that spewed out waste from the local brewery, and this was a hotspot for roach, which we caught using hempseed as bait. We fed the swim with hempseed, too, which was kept in a linen bag. The shank of the hooks we painted white to look like shoots emerging from the seeds, and we had to use lead wire in place of split shot otherwise the roach would try to swallow the shot, mistaking it for hempseed! Sometimes when the fish were in a feeding frenzy we could even get away with using a small piece of rubber tubing as bait. And often, when fishing for roach in the winter my tutors would chuck out a roach livebait on a huge FG pike bung, most days managing to catch a pike or two.

'A man for all seasons' would be a good title for Tony Miles, a modern-day angler who, like me, was a disciple of Walker and has gone a long way to catch fish like the master. He is a very successful angler on rivers and still-waters, with several books to his credit: the one on chub fishing could well become the bible for all those who seek this species. Tony is another of the 'nice guys' in angling today and, although he has an enviable record of big fish, he still holds down an exhausting job selling life assurance with a multi-national company. He has also found a way of having a happy family life and a fishing career. He takes his wife Fran and their children on holiday two or three times a year, they have a lovely home in the West Midlands, and he finds time to care about others less fortunate than himself. For example, some time ago a lady in his office was diagnosed as having multiple sclerosis; Tony took the trouble to phone me for advice, and I was able to send him some books written for those who have MS.

SEA FISHING MEMORIES

I have probably had the best sea fishing that anyone could wish for. At Dungeness, Hythe, Dover, Deal, Folkstone and Ramsgate I have fished from boats, piers and beaches; those were days when cod reigned supreme in the winter months, when during the summer we caught plaice with spots as big as half-crowns, thornback rays, dabs by the hundred – what a lovely-tasting fish they are – and lots of mackerel, which were great fun on light spinning tackle.

One Friday morning in July 1962 I received a call from John MacDonald at Deal. 'Can you get down? I've found a mussel bed that's covered in plaice.' I said I could, and asked him to get me ten score of yellow tails – the local lugworm, highly prized by anglers and fish alike. John replied that he had already got me a bucketful of fresh lug, as he had guessed I would come down once I heard the news about the plaice. I planned my campaign. It was going to be a neap tide so I could use light tackle, which meant leads of between 4 oz and 6oz, a line of 20lb breaking strain, a small Penn multiplier reel and my Milbro Neptune boat rod. We – that is Frank Edmonds, Arthur Sayers and I – arrived at Deal in plenty of time. We parked the van and went along to Jim Heard's tackle shop to pick up a few bits and pieces (isn't it amazing how we always end up having to buy tackle we already have back at home?), then it was in to the café for tea and toast, and there John joined us.

The weather was kind to us, with a light wind and a warm sun: perfect! Days like that make up for the ones when either you have to hold on with one hand for fear of being blown overboard, or you can't even get afloat. Once in the boat, a clinker-built job that had the engine in the centre, we slid down the shingle bank and into the sea. It was a half-hour trip to the mussel bed, and during that time we set up our tackle. Our end rig was a spreader made from stainless steel, with two size 2/0 fine wire, long-shank Aberdeen hooks baited with yellow tails. We were ready!

Once over the mark, down went the anchor, and after a couple of minutes John said, 'Okay, it's all yours!' I put the spool out of gear and lowered the baited hooks to the sea bed, then flicked the reel back into gear. I must have waited all of ten seconds when I felt a fish mouth the bait, and then another one: I struck, and winched up two plaice each around two pounds. It was as easy as that! I rebaited and dropped the tackle down again, and soon two more fish were being brought in. Frank and Arthur were doing just as well, and that's how the fishing was for the next three hours, with some of the plaice weighing over four pounds. We put back those under two pounds whenever they were lip-hooked. It was wonderful sport: plaice fishing at its best.

By eight o'clock we had had enough, and headed for shore. We booked the boat for the next afternoon, but that trip was to be a disaster because a trawler went over the mussel bed early in the morning and scraped it clean. Between the three of us we had just two bites from small dogfish.

BEACH FISHING

Although I enjoyed my boat fishing, I considered beach fishing for cod on a winter's night far better. It wasn't so much for the amount of fish one caught but the skill needed to do well; not to mention the friends one made. Dungeness was the place I enjoyed most of all, and I had a good arrangement with an old trawler fishing family, the Oilers, who would supply me with black lugworm whenever I wanted.

Dungeness is a gravel spit sticking out into the English Channel, a desolate place in those days, with a lifeboat and just a few trawlers which doubled as angling boats. The most famous beach-fishing mark was known as The Dustbin, and fishing there required long-range casting. Two men who could always reach the mark were Tom Hutchinson and Les Moncrief; Les was another gentle giant and a most generous man.

Through my friend Frank Edmonds, I would get to know when Les and Tom would be fishing and arrange to join them. I spent more time watching these two in action than fishing myself; but it was well worth it, and slowly with their teaching my casting improved. With their help I could sometimes cast my bait into The Dustbin even at high water, and not just when the tide was out (which of course was a shorter cast). My catches improved with my casting, and soon I could get a few cod on most tides, although I must have spent many hours on the field at the back of our house perfecting my casting and getting ribald remarks from dog-walkers.

BIG COD

My best cod didn't come from my favourite fishing spot of Dungeness, but from a boat-fishing trip out from Deal; it was one of those lucky fish which we catch now and then, as I wasn't fishing for cod but for thornback rays. It was around four o'clock in the afternoon, the tide was flooding and conditions seemed perfect for rays. I was fishing with a 20lb line class rod, 24lb breaking strain line and a size 4/0 hook on some 30lb breaking strain nylon trace. I don't like to use wire when fishing for rays; I think it's a mistake to do so. With an 8-foot flowing trace and a fillet of mackerel as bait bouncing well away from the boat, I lifted the rod to work the bait a bit further down the tide, and the rod was pulled down savagely. There was no need to strike, for the fish had hooked itself and was trying to move downtide. Grudgingly the reel gave line and I felt the fish shake its head in an effort to get rid of the hook. This was no ray: it was a fish that could fight a bit . . . cod? Everyone agreed it had to be. I began to get some line back on the reel. This wasn't the sort of fish that could strip line off a reel like a bonefish, salmon, carp or pike, but it was a dogged fighter.

Slowly I pumped the fish towards the boat; then it surfaced about ten yards from the stern, and I gasped. It was hooked lightly in the scissors, a big fish, thirty pounds I thought. It opened its mouth, the tide flooded in and the fish went below the surface. I continued pumping and then suddenly it was there, alongside the boat. It looked huge. Brian put the net under it and scooped it out: it was mine! The big cod coughed up four crabs and a partially digested flatfish; we put it on the scales and they pulled down to 28lb 7oz. I was thrilled.

BACK TO SCHOOL

Fly casting has always been a problem for me. I taught myself to fly fish when I was about fifteen years old because I wanted to catch wild brown trout from the Darenth during the close season for coarse fish. For many years I thought I could cast but then realized I was awful at the job and needed to improve, and so a few years ago I visited the West Wales School of Flyfishing under the tutorship of Pat O'Reilly and Derek Hoskin. That started what was for me a long friendship with both families, but as teachers how they coped with me I shall never know, because they had to overcome thirty-odd years of bad habits. However, I feel now, at the age of fifty-six, that I can cast well enough to be let loose on such famous rivers as the Deschutes and the Umpqua in Oregon. And I would say to anyone who hasn't attended a professional fly-fishing school, try to do so. Learn from the experts who know how to teach. Your best mate might be the best angler around, but there's a world of difference between being a good angler and being a good teacher. Kate and I benefited from lessons from two of the very best anglers and teachers.

SKIFFLE GROUP

The fifties were the days of rock and roll, Teddy boys and skiffle groups; of Bill Hayley, Elvis Presley and Tommy Steel; and for me, Soho coffee bars and girlfriends. Living in a Medway town meant it was quite easy to get a train to Charing Cross for a night on the town, then come back on the milk train in the early hours of the morning to change and be ready for a day's work. I was no different from the rest of the lads: I had my full drape jacket with a velvet collar, my drainpipe trousers and brothel-creeper shoes.

One day during the close season my mates and I were sitting in a coffee bar trying to find something to occupy our minds when Brian Smithers said, 'Let's form a skiffle group'. We told him it was a daft idea because we had none of the gear, but he replied that he had a guitar and that we could make all the rest. I was doubtful and asked what was the point of it all, to which Smithers responded that there was a competition for groups at The Majestic and entry was free.

We had Smithers on guitar; Paul Clements on a double bass made from a tea chest, a broom handle and a piece of thin cord; and me on washboard. The idea was doomed from the start because none of us could sing, but going on stage at least got the girls talking to us afterwards. We got nowhere, of course, but it was fun.

CARP CATCH

It was in 1957 that I caught thirteen double-figure carp in a single session at Paddlesworth lake using potato bait. All through the close season I visited the claypit every day, throwing in boiled potatoes to educate the fish into taking them. I dug the bank out to make a small cave, and had a trench system from my chosen spot to those of Pete Tillitt and Bill Cutting. I had become friendly with the foreman of the cement works nearby, and he gave me a key to their hut where there was an electric kettle and a stove. On cold wet nights we used to sleep in the hut.

We raked the swims, dumping in a load of gravel that we got from the gravel works at Leybourne, and we kept feeding our swims with potatoes, keeping the matter a secret from everyone else. The plan was that Peter and I would fish for two weeks from the start of the season, with Bill joining us at weekends.

I arrived at the pit on the afternoon of the first day and found that only two carp had been caught. Moving into my chosen area I tackled up with two Mk IV carp rods matched with Mitchell 300 reels and 11lb Sportex Perlon camouflage line. I was going to use size 4 Model Perfect hooks which I had been given by an old angler who no longer went fishing. I positioned my Heron bite indicators and used a baiting needle to pull the line through the potato; then I tied on the hook with a piece of crust on the bend to stop it pulling through the soft potato. I can't understand how anglers in the past fished with so-called parboiled potatoes, as I find it almost impossible to pull the hook through when striking unless the potatoes are boiled until they are soft enough to eat. I cast out both rods and sat back to await events. Five minutes later I was into my first fish, a mirror carp of about ten pounds, and then soon after I had another much the same size. It seemed that all the hard work was paying off.

But alas, that was my lot, and I had no more takes that night or through the next day. Then as we sat having our evening meal late that day, I asked Bill and Pete if they could smell carp. They laughed, but I have always found that when the carp are going to feed you get a smell like water mint. Nothing happened until dawn the next morning, and then the silver paper on one of my rods shot up to the butt ring. Line peeled off the spool, I struck, and a fish was on. As I was playing this fish the indicator on my other rod was away. I bent down, banged the pick-up in and struck: the second fish was on, so I opened the bale arm and dropped the rod. Bill was there to net the first fish, a nice double of about twelve pounds, so I picked up the second rod and that fish was still on. Soon carp number two was landed, another double like the first. We put them into submerged sacks for weighing later.

I rebaited both rods and cast out just a few yards. I could see carp rooting around in the bottom, no doubt looking for spuds. I chucked a few out and we made a brew, but before I could finish mine one of the rods was away. The carp kept coming: it was an incredible fishing session. As I fished on, Peter weighed some of the fish because we didn't have enough sacks, even though other anglers loaned me theirs. In four hours I landed thirteen doubles, the best weighing 12lb 10oz; then they stopped biting and I went another two days without catching a fish.

During the week another angler saw me catch a fish, and when I landed it the potato was still on the line. He asked what it was and I said 'It's a new type of weight made from wood so that it sinks slowly and lies on the weed'. He accepted my explanation, so our secret bait was safe for a little bit longer.

WINTER BREAM FISHING

Living in Kent in the fifties, I was lucky to have the best bream fishing in the country on the River Beault. Two people who really knew how to fish for bream were Brian Holloway and Tony How, and they were particularly successful on mild winter days when the river was bank high or dropping after a flood. Their style of fishing, which I copied, was quite simple: they used 16-foot Clarkson of Rochester three-piece rods with whole cane butts and two sections of split bamboo. Their reels were Rapidex centre-pins filled with 6lb line, they used size 6 hooks, and their bait consisted of big pieces of crust or flake, or a lobworm which they fished by a method known as float legering, or laying-on. The float was a big goose or swan quill, and a bored bullet was stopped about twelve inches from the hook.

Favoured swims were slower water on the inside of a bend, a big eddy, or places where the water flowed deep and fairly fast but without those whirlpools that you often find when the river is fining down after a flood. Having plumbed the depth, the float was set about two feet over-depth. We would have to bait our swims quite heavily with mashed bread bran and chopped worms, made into cricket-ball size. We threw in three or four balls to start with, and a couple more each time we caught a fish.

The Beault was rated the best winter bream river in the south-east of England (the best in the country, we thought), and around Hunton was probably the best. It was deep and twisting, a real Crabtree river with lots of willows and the odd big oak whose roots stretched far out into the water. On 14 March 1954, the last day of the season, I was on the river at Hunton some 1,200 yards upstream of the road bridge, in a small copse. The weather was mild but cloudy with showers, and the river was just fining down after a flood: perfect for big bream.

I tackled up for laying on, using 4lb line, a swan quill float and a bored bullet stopped some 18 inches from a size 6 hook. My bait was a lively lobworm, my favourite for fishing in coloured water. I fed four balls of mashed bread, bran and chopped worms into the swim, and cast out so that the tackle swung round and lay downstream of the rod tip. Then I put the rod in the rest and sat back to await events. Two hours later I had my first bream, a fish of about four pounds; then a couple of pound perch, followed by three more bream around the four-pound mark. It was looking good. Then the float sank slowly out of sight, and I lifted the rod and tightened into a good fish; these river bream could really pull your string and bend your stick. After a fair bit of pulling and boring the fish swirled on the surface and came to the net; it was a bream of around five pounds. I thought it was my biggest ever, and placed the fish in the keepnet so that I could get the weighing scales.

It was a long run to the Bull pub where the club scales were kept, and I was quite breathless when I arrived.

'Can I have the scales please, mister?' I asked.

'What have you caught, then?' the pub owner asked, and I told him it was a big bream. 'I'll be right with you,' he told me. He fetched the scales and we made our back to the river where he set them up on the bank while I got the net out of the water.

'That's a big 'un, boy,' the landlord said. And it was . . . 5lb 4oz, my best-ever bream and on the very last day of the season.

Since then I've had quite a few good fish on the last day of the season, including a 3lb perch, a 6lb chub, a 22lb pike and a 2lb roach.

CREAM OF ROACH FISHING

In the fifties and early sixties the River Medway provided some of the best roach fishing in the country. During autumn and winter the fishing was excellent, and not at all difficult if you followed the simple rules of keeping quiet and fishing the bait on or near the bottom. In normal conditions the Medway was a deep, slow-flowing river with big shoals of quality roach. The best fishing was between Yalding and East Farleigh. It wasn't a river with a gravel bottom and water-crowfoot beds with those lovely white buttercups we see on the southern chalk streams; the Medway flows through Kentish clay and there is very little weed apart from the odd patch of waterlilies and sedges lining the margins here and there. It was in these weedier places that we would seek the winter roach.

On the railway side of the river, notably from the high bank downstream of Yalding to Nettlestead and from Barming Bridge down to East Farleigh where most of our fishing was done, much of the bank was tree-lined and there were lots of stinging nettles, blackberry bushes and elderberry trees. I loved the weir pools at Yalding, Teston and Farleigh. At Teston weir, on the right-hand bank of the pool, there were some old ruins where we used to camp in the summer. This was my favourite place. Just below the weir is a lovely old stone bridge where you could stand in summer and watch shoals of fish darting for scraps of food. Further downstream were some hawthorn bushes, and beneath it a wonderful roach swim holding lots of 1lb-plus fish and the occasional two-pounder.

Medway roach anglers eagerly awaited the first floods of autumn when the surging muddy water would sweep away all the rubbish left by summer visitors and hop pickers. This was the land of hops, and just upstream of Yalding at East Peckham were Whitbread brewery's oast houses where every year hundreds of East Enders came to pick hops and have a good time. Lots of the hop pickers were roach anglers who brought with them their black wooden seat-boxes and Sowerbutts roach poles. Most of them used hemp for feeding and bait. There was many a brief love affair between the East London girls and the Kentish lads; when we went fishing for the weekend we took a change of clothes so that we could go to the pubs and dances around East Peckham, Yalding, Nettlestead and Wateringbury.

Enough of this . . . let's get back to the roach, a favourite fish not just of the Kentish anglers but also of Londoners who came in coachloads on Sunday mornings. You would see them sweeping across the fields to their favourite swims, lovely people, always willing to help and share their knowledge with us. I made many friends and sometimes a couple of them would fish on a Saturday and stay the night at my house. We would all go off to the Pavilion dance hall at Gillingham on the Saturday evening, and fish again on the Sunday. This way they had two days' fishing for the price of one.

In the fifties, four styles of fishing were popular with Medway roach anglers: swimming the stream, legering, float legering and laying-on. The top baits were bread crust, flake and paste, gentles and lobworms, although occasionally we did use such baits as hempseed, stewed wheat and cheese. When the river was carrying two feet of extra water, anglers would fish with 10- or 12-foot rods and centre-pin reels, but now and again you would see someone with a fixed-spool reel such as an Omnia, a reel that looked like a cycle dynamo.

With the river at its normal winter level we used float tackle, either swimming or trotting the stream, although some anglers still fished with the old Thames-style roach pole with great success, and I enjoyed watching them as they fed with hempseed and fished with hemp or an elderberry on the hook.

I had some great bags of pound-plus roach on lobworm bait when the river was in flood. One February day I was at Teston, downstream of the bridge; the river was over the fields, and the road on the approach to the bridge was under water. I fished laying-on style with lobworm bait in front of some half-submerged hawthorn bushes, and caught seventeen roach all over the pound mark, the best making 1lb 12oz, as well as several bream around three pounds and a few eels.

Another time I had gone by train to Yalding and walked downriver to the start of the trees on the high bank. It was a frosty November morning, the river had some flow and colour, and the puddles on the field were thick with ice. I didn't think much of my chances. The swim I chose, in front of some withered brown sedges, was around eight feet deep. I fished laying on, with a 16-foot rod with whole cane butt with a split bamboo middle and top joint, Rapidex centre-pin reel and 3lb line. Four BB shot were bunched twelve inches from the hook, and my bait was flake on a size 8 hook. It was not until around two o'clock in the afternoon that I had my first bite, a pound-plus roach; this was followed by a couple of bream, and then six bites and six good roach. The frost was coming down now, and my fingers were getting numb;

rooks, crows and pigeons were going to roost, and there was the occasional sound of gunshot. The sky overhead was electric blue, and in the direction of the setting sun it was pink and orange, a sure sign that there would be a heavy frost. A pheasant crowed from the tree behind me as it went to roost. I would stick it out until dark, and maybe do an extra half an hour with my cycle lamp beamed onto the float.

I changed over to crust and moved the shot down to within three inches of the hook; then, in a magnificent couple of hours fishing into the darkness, I had a succession of pound-plus roach and two 4lb bream. Every cast brought me a fish. I ended the day with twenty-six big roach, the best weighing 1lb 14oz. I didn't want to pack up, but the cold was so intense that I couldn't stand it any longer. Nevertheless I was a happy angler as I trudged upriver to Yalding station, thinking of the warm train carriage and of checking my football pools when I got the evening paper at Maidstone.

I used the same method on another chilly day when the banks at Nettlestead were covered with frozen snow and cat ice fringed the margins. I was with Brian Long who lived in Strood, and to help us contend with the cold we had a bottle of brandy. I chose a swim in front of some waterlilies, and my hook-bait was bread cube. For a long time we saw not a sign of a fish, and as we chatted the level of the brandy bottle fell steadily. Eventually my float slowly slipped from sight, and an answering strike brought me a good roach. By the time it got dark I had caught several nice roach, including three over the two-pound mark. It had been a good day.

We arrived back at Strood station a little worse for wear, having consumed all the brandy. Brian, who was married, had invited me back to his home for a meal, but it was gone 8.30 p.m. when we staggered up the garden path. Brian knocked at the door, and it was answered by a woman's voice which screamed, 'Here's your bloody dinner.' – and she threw it at him. I decided not to stay!

CHAPTER 4

Branching Out

The Kingfisher

Resplendent in his coat of blue,
Complete with royal crown,
Perched on leafy bough he waits,
Poised without a sound,
Eyes alert upon the flow,
The river running by,
He has no need for rod and line,
No use for bait or fly.
King of all the fishermen,
He casts his vision wide,
Then dives with ease to lift his catch,
Triumphant with his prize.
Orange and purple, blue and green,
Colours clear and bright,
One of Nature's gentlemen,
Majestic in his flight,
Day by day he reigns supreme,
The grassy bank his home,
The riverside his palace grounds,
The hanging trees his throne.

Lorraine Davies

The world's biggest-selling angling newspaper, *Angling Times*, was first published in July 1953. It was a beautiful morning in Kent: the sun was shining, the sky was blue, and a few white clouds like puffs of smoke drifted by as I queued up outside the newsagent's at five-thirty in the morning to get my copy of the first edition. I went in as the newsagent was undoing bundles of papers.

'Can I have my *Angling Times*, please?' I asked.

'Well, you'll have to wait while I serve these other customers,' he told me.

'No, I won't,' I said, 'I was here before them, and I want my *Angling Times*, please.'

He said, 'They're all still bundled up.' So I told him, 'Then you will have to unbundle 'em, because I want my *Angling Times*,' and I gave him my fourpence. On the front page there was a kingfisher motif, and I decided, there and then, that when I got my own place it would be called 'Kingfisher'.

Bernard Venables, of Mr Crabtree fame, was the editorial director, Colin Willock was the editor, and we had this great man Dick Walker writing his full-page feature 'Walker's Pitch.' As a publicity campaign, *Angling Times* released tagged perch into waters up and down the country; if you caught one of these tagged fish you would win up to £25, which was a lot of money then. My friends and I were there when Bernard Venables came down to the River Medway at Tonbridge to release some of these perch. There was our hero, Crabtree of *Daily Mirror* fame. Clutching my autograph book I got close enough to say, 'Good morning, sir,' but I was too shy to ask him for his autograph. My mates kept saying, 'Go on, go and ask him.'

'I can't,' I said nervously, 'That's Mr Crabtree.' He was just how I had pictured him.

In his writing in *Angling Times*, Bernard Venables talked about going to the Norfolk Broads to catch big pike and rudd. This whetted my appetite for the Broads, especially when he described the reed-fringed waters where the big pike lurked: Dudgeon's Corner, Heigham Sound, Candle Dyke, Hickling Broad and Potter Heigham – what romantic names they were to us young anglers. They evoked visions of huge pike, dustbin-lid sized bream, golden-bodied rudd with blood-red fins, and those lovely fish of high summer, the tench. But what appealed to me most of all was the pike, a perfect predator that has been around for millions of years.

MEDWAY PIKE

I had caught pike up to fifteen pounds in various waters including the Rivers Medway, Beault and Kentish Stour as well as in gravel- and clay pits. At that time my most memorable pike was a 10½lb fish I caught at the age of thirteen while fishing at Teston weir. It was my first double, and quite a story in itself: I was fishing the weir pool for chub, using my Wallis Wizard rod with whole cane butt and split bamboo middle and top joints. I had already caught a few chub when I saw all these little fish jumping out of the water; it was just as Mr Crabtree had shown us in his *Daily Mirror* cartoon strip.

'Ah,' I thought. 'A pike!' And I really wanted to catch that pike.

I brought my tackle in and made up a rig with a *Fishing Gazette* pike 'bung' – they were real big old things; nothing sensitive about them – and a Jardine snap tackle. The snap tackle was simply a pair of treble hooks on a wire trace. Then I grabbed myself a little gudgeon for bait from the keepnet and chucked this lot out where the pike was. It had only been out there for about four or five minutes when the float went under. Before striking, you either had to sing the first chorus of 'God Save The King', or count to ten; at least, that's what we used to think. Being a Royalist, I always sang the chorus. I tightened into what I considered was this huge monster; and played it out.

An angler further down the river bank shouted to me, 'D'you need any help sonny?'

'Yes please, mister,' I yelled back.

He came up and gaffed the fish for me (this is something we would never do nowadays; we are much more careful in handling fish). At that time we didn't have landing nets big enough for pike, so we used to gaff them under the jaw. We got the fish onto the bank and the man said, 'What do you want to do with it?'

'I'm taking it home for my mum,' I told him. He weighed it for me on an old brass spring balance and said it was 10½lb. Well, I was so excited I couldn't fish any more, so I packed up and dragged my tackle and the pike down to the bridge which was a couple of hundred yards from the weir pool. I put the rods along the crossbar and the tackle box on the back, and then I thought, 'What am I going to do with this pike?' So I found a bit of string, and tied the head of the fish to my handlebars; the tail was just dragging on the ground, and like that I had to cycle back to Strood.

As I was coming through Snodland a man stopped me and asked if I wanted to sell my salmon. I said, 'This ain't a salmon, mister. This is a pike, and I ain't going to sell it. I'm taking it home for my mum.' When I got home my mother called all the neighbours round to see the big pike. 'Look what my boy's caught,' she told them. This was in the days of rationing, and so we gave pike cutlets to some of our neighbours.

When I look back on that incident I realize that killing the pike was wrong, but then we were not educated as to how we should care for and protect our fish. Nowadays, of course, we gently return our catch to the water. This episode was the start of my interest in pike, the fish they used to call the 'river wolf' or 'freshwater shark'. I was just a youngster, and these were big fish: they pulled back when you tried to bring them in. If a pike wanted to go the other way, it was always a struggle. I could imagine myself as a big game angler when I went after pike, and of course on the Norfolk Broads you could catch twenty-pounders.

NORFOLK BROADS

I went up to the Broads with Paul Bryant with whom I sometimes fished on the Medway, Thames and Beault. Paul worked in the Chatham dockyard where he could make big metal rings for our special keepnets. The netting itself was made up by an old Dungeness fisherman. These keepnets were 8 feet long and about 3 feet in diameter: they were massive.

If we had any spare money it always went on tackle. We had good quality split bamboo rods and lovely centre-pin reels; I also had a pair of Mitchell 300 fixed spool reels, bought for me by my parents. But my pride and joy was a Felton cross-wind fixed spool reel of a type Richard Walker had written about; and if Richard Walker used it then we had to use it, because he had proved to us that you could catch big fish by design and not just by luck.

I had my old walnut and brass star-back reel which was a delight to use, and an unusual rod I sometimes fished with for pike which was actually a billiard cue fitted with white porcelain-lined rings. I used it mainly for my cod fishing, but it doubled as a pike rod when I needed a second outfit. Some of us still used the old silk lines. These were woven and had to be well look after, and during a day's fishing they might have to be greased every half hour or so to keep them afloat; also, when you got home you would have to take all the line off the reel and put it onto a line winder. I couldn't afford to buy one of these, so I made one out of a cycle wheel. The grease we used was Mucilin, which is still available today for use on modern lines. We also had ICI Luron, the first of the nylon lines, although mainly we used cuttyhunk line, usually a dirty brown colour and a bit like string. It, too, had to be greased often to keep it floating. Cuttyhunk was horrible stuff to fish with, but we used it because it was cheap.

The night before we left on our Norfolk Broads expedition we went to the local bakery and got a sack of stale loaves to use as groundbait for the rudd, tench and bream. With this, our suitcases, tackle boxes, tent and paraffin lamps, we were well loaded down as we made our way to the railway station. From Strood we went to London and then changed trains for Great Yarmouth. What a struggle we had with all that gear! On the journey up to Great Yarmouth we talked about some of the famous people who fished the Norfolk Broads. One of these was a river board bailiff called Dennis Pye. We had seen pictures of Dennis, wearing an old peaked cap and sitting in his little boat with its Seagull outboard motor, and his big Alsatian dog which used to stand proudly in the bow.

In the fifties Great Yarmouth was a hive of activity. There were herring smacks in the harbour, and in the dock area you could buy fresh herrings and have them packed in a box and sent off to any address you wanted. They also did kippers, and so I had a box sent home to my mother, another to Aunt Peg and also one to Granny; I always looked after Granny, because if I did, my grandfather used to take me fishing in his car and then I didn't have to worry about catching trains!

It was quite a few miles to Martham, and we decided to take a taxi; it cost five shillings, and this meant we had to scrounge food for a day or two. At

Martham there used to be an old ferry across the River Thurne, which you operated yourself, by pulling on a chain. On one side of the ferry was a boat-yard, and on the other a little dyke where boats were moored. Above the dyke was a field with a well in one corner, and this provided us with drinking water. We decided to camp on the river bank. We didn't have a proper tent; in fact my ground sheet was an old army camouflaged gas cape, and the tent was just a piece of canvas draped over the wooden framework of a couple of forked sticks with a branch lying across the forks – we really were quite poor!

At Martham ferry we met a great big man with a hunched back; his name was George Gallant, and he was a very kind and gentle old man. He had a little green shed next to the boatyard, and he used to hire out dinghies to anglers. From this shed he also used to sell tinned food and all sorts of other goods. On the first day I went to him and said, 'Hello Mr Gallant, sir.' (We called everybody 'sir' or 'madam', of course, and always with a 'Mr' or 'Mrs' until you were told you didn't have to.)

'Oh,' he said. 'You don't call me "sir", boy. You call me "Mr Gallant." '

We asked where the best fishing was, and were told Dudgeon's Corner, Heigham Sound, Candle Dyke and so on – all the places we had read about and really wanted to go to.

A few days later I went to George and said, 'I need a new battery for my torch, please George.' By that time we were on really friendly terms and were calling each other by our Christian names. He was a bit like a father to us.

'You want a what, boy?'

'I want a battery.'

'And what's that, then?' he asked. I showed him my torch.

'Ah!' he said. 'You want a *bartery*.' And I said, 'Er, yes, that's right.'

I got a 'bartery', which was important because there was a storm brewing. But George said, 'You boys can't stay in the tent – there'll be bad flooding tonight. Here's the key to my shed; you can sleep in there.' And we did, which was remarkable when you think of it because he had all his tinned food and other stock in that shed and yet he trusted us to sleep there. But that was the way things were in those days.

We fished all through the night and caught bream, big fish of around four pounds, and we probably had a dozen apiece as well as lots of eels. As soon as you put a worm in the water it seemed there were a million eels around it. We unhooked and released most of these, though always kept back a few because a plate of fried eels used to go down very well for breakfast, and we didn't have much to spend on food: we were spending most of our money on bait.

Sometimes we would catch a big tench on a piece of bread flake at dusk or dawn, but strangely we never caught these fish during the night. My best tench weighed in at 5lb 4oz. Bread was also the best bait for the bream, and had the advantage that it didn't attract the eels.

Occasionally we would go off in the dinghy at dawn and creep up Heigham

Sound in search of big rudd. We would anchor hairnets filled with bread in likely looking spots in the hope of drawing the rudd out of the reeds, as Mr Crabtree had taught us. It was a very successful way of fishing. The tackle was quite simple: an Avon-type rod, fixed spool reel and greased line. The bait was bread flake which we would cast towards the anchored bread whenever we spotted the rudd feeding. If the water was choppy then we would use a float and fish the bread about six inches under the surface. Paul and I both caught rudd over two pounds using these methods.

We had these cherry pipes in which we tried to burn shag tobacco. However, probably because we sat there concentrating on our fishing, we could never keep the cherry pipes going so it was costing us a fortune in matches.

On the third morning I was lying back in the tent, tired but happy after fishing all night. We had caught a fair few bream while using a torch to light up the float, and they had been super bites, too, with the float sliding away out of the torch beam. I must have dropped off to sleep, and it was perhaps about ten o'clock in the morning when I woke up lying on my back. I was trying to focus my eyes when I saw this monster sitting on my tummy. I blinked and thought, 'What the hell's that?'

Suddenly I realized it was a coypu rat. Well, I had been told that these rats were fearsome and dangerous creatures, and here was this great big one sitting on me and holding a hunk of bread. I thought , 'Er, what do I do now?' But my tummy muscles must have tightened and transmitted my fear to the coypu, because it bounded out of our bivvy and crashed into the water. It had certainly given me a bit of a scare, but I told myself, 'I've had a coypu sitting on me, and not everyone can say that!'

The next night Paul and I were sitting in the boat fishing; we had caught some bream and were watching our bite indicators by the light of a hurricane lamp. Suddenly a coypu jumped off the bank – I suppose it didn't realize we were there – and crashed into our boat. All hell was let loose. We didn't know what to do. Should we jump into the river, or try to clamber up the bank? Thankfully the coypu was more afraid than we were. It hopped and ran about the boat for what seemed like ages but was probably only seconds, and then dived into the water. But that was quite enough for us. It was probably about two o'clock in the morning, and we decided we would go and have a brew and get our heads down rather than fish any more that night.

The following night we agreed that we wouldn't fish; but come midnight we had overcome our fear of coypu rats, and decided that it would be a better bet to fish from the boat where we could reach further out into the water with our floats.

We had no more problems with coypu; in fact we quite enjoyed seeing them around, and they almost became our friends. Sadly you don't see coypu on the Broads these days, although they are still common in France where I see them

Sir Winston Churchill inspects wartime damage. (Photo courtesy of the Master and Fellows of Churchill College, Cambridge.)

Barnes and Mortlake Angling Society coach trip to Britford on the Hampshire Avon in 1950. Club secretary Bill Drake, centre, is seen here with two committee members.

Richard Walker in his study perusing his Stillwater Angling, *a book that changed the future of fishing.*

The front page of the first issue of Angling Times.

ALLCOCKS
REDDITCH. ENGLAND.

ANGLING TIMES

TRADE MARKS
ALLCOCKS
REDDITCH. ENGLAND.

No. 1   **FRIDAY, JULY 10, 1953**   PRICE 4d.   Postage 1½d.

A Competition for Every Angler

ERCH WITH A PRICE ON HEIR HEADS

Bernard Venables to start new-style angling contest

Cash For Anglers
Aid For A.C.A.

ON Saturday, July 25, at a well-known water as yet kept secret, Bernard Venables, Editorial Director of the "Angling Times," will start a brand new kind of angling competition that will set fishermen the length and breadth of England talking.

The competition, for which large cash prizes will be given, will take place throughout the season, and in places up and down the country, at three weekly intervals. And this is the way it will be . . . .

On Saturday, July 25, at a time later to be announced, Bernard Venables will arrive at the selected fishing station in the ANGLING TIMES van.

In the back of the van, in well-aerated tanks, will be fifty perch in the prime of life.

Each of these perch will carry in its left opercular bone, or gill-cover, a small metal tag. This will have been fixed there in a manner approved by the Fresh-water Biological Association and the Ministry of Agriculture and Fisheries.

Venables will then release the perch in batches of five at a time into anglers' favourite swims on that stretch of the river.

After that, it is up to the anglers present to land them.

There is no time limit. The beauty of the competition is that novice and expert stand an equal chance. Expensive tackle will have little bearing on success.

The first perch caught will bring its captor £50.

The second wins £10; the third, £5; the fourth, £3. Every subsequent fish earns a 5s. tackle voucher.

But that is not all.

By the rules of the competition, the angler benefits not only himself but his sport.

For every marked fish landed, the "Angling Times" will give £3 to the A.C.A. to help in its fight against pollution.

Week by week we shall inform readers how many of these fish have been landed, and what prizes remain to be claimed.

No part of the country will be neglected.

Next week we shall announce the location of the first release of Prize Perch.

Anglers are cordially invited to watch Bernard Venables set loose the fish that may mean that the next bob of the float will bring £20. WHERE?

See Next Week's Announcement

PRIZE PERCH RULES

1 Remove metal tag from gill-cover carefully, without damaging the fish. (See picture)

2 Return the fish to the water having taken care to handle it throughout with wet hands

3 Post the tag to "Angling Times," 4 Breams Buildings, E.C.4, enclosing coupon to be published next week

4 DO NOT SEND US THE FISH. Violation of this rule means instant disqualification

Mansized Mullet

SUCCESS came to G. E. Bowding after a three-day attempt to catch a large mullet off the rocks near Portland Bill.

Bowding noted a grey mullet swimming lazily near some weed-covered rocks east of the Bill.

On the third day of concentrated fishing the mullet—6lb 2½oz.—fell to bread paste.

BOY CATCHES CATFISH

A 27½ lb. Danubian catfish, landed after a half-hour fight by a 16-year-old Leighton Buzzard angler, Peter Bassett, not only topped the record of catfish caught in this club's water this season so far, but left the rod used with a permanent bend.

Peter made his catch in the Middle Lake at Claydon Park, near Winslow, in the early hours of a Sunday morning. The fish measured 30 inches in length and was eight inches across the head. Tackle included an 8lb. b.s. line and No. 6 hook. Witnesses who applauded Peter's effort included J. Brennan, resident bailiff, and J. Jennings,

honorary bailiff to the Great Ouse River Board.

The first catfish to be caught in this club's water this season fell to a worm offered by C. S. Lloyd, of Great Horwood. J. Brennan weighed the fish, which topped the scales at 19½ and measured 42½ inches in length. This one took twenty minutes to land on a 7lb. b.s. line and No. 10 hook.

Members estimate that the largest catfish—introduced into the lakes by the Club—should weigh up to 40lb. Large carp, bream, and rare American perch have also been introduced. The lakes are famous for their fine tench.

W' twelve days after the g of the coarse fishing anglers in the Bristol offered a heavy blow when on killed fish in a three-retch of the Avon.

ollution hits stol Avon

estimated that between rs and 15,000 roach, dace, and pike died. Fortunately only the stretch of the river n Hanham and Netham was affected and the river Hanham weir is still e.

HIGH TIDE

morning of June 28 a tide—but not an exception—held back the fresh that flowed between the eirs and pushed back up ds Hanham sewage that rs into this stretch.

oupled with the exception—a high water temperature riped in a bit of rain, was rning point to pollution. temperature was said to ound 80 degrees Fahren-

fishes so well today—last on some contests 12lb. of as needed for a win — is the efforts of the Avon vation and Re-stocking y.

RE-STOCKING

hen the Society has re-d with a quarter of a n fish of all species officials, including D. E. rr, Pollution and Fisheries ector, Bath, and Water T. Dyer, of Bristol, were on the scene in the polluted

s of water were taken fish were taken to the ys officials of the Avon

EEDED OFF

d-cutting operations the-sport in Kettering ation's match for the spon Shield, fished by 14 s of foul in the Titchmarsh waters. Swims where the e had not reached pro-the winners

ult: 1. N. Spring's team ts: 2. R. Knight (13-5-2): 3. ns (11-2-4)

Another big fish from the mighty Amazon river.

Artist, wildfowler and writer 'BB' (Dennis Watkins-Pitchford) with Polar.

Well-known angler, writer, broadcaster and shooting man Hugh Falkus.

Picture of my son Nigel; even as a young lad he enjoyed field sports. Here, pictured waiting to move off to a grouse moor for a day's shooting.

No wheelchair was going to stop me from shooting.

We often take calls from listeners before going on air.

Re-living the past: fishing with old cane rods on the River Kennet.

Tony Miles and I discuss Wensum chub fishing for my radio programme Hook Line and Sinker.

With tackle over my shoulder and walking frame at the ready, I am off to the River Ribble in search of winter chub.

when I am fishing. It seems this South American rodent is still very much at home in Europe.

Once, when we were fishing Heigham Sound for rudd, there was a huge eruption and boil on the surface: we saw a greeny-yellow shape, and knew that pike were around. All the stories of the huge monsters of the Broads came flooding back into our minds, the tales we had been told up in the tavern about these big pike, and we decided to fish for them.

They were not easy to catch, and there were lots of problems: the water wasn't very deep and it was very weedy, and we kept getting our baits caught up. We were still fishing livebaits in those days, and they kept swimming into the reeds and the weed. We caught a few pike to about eight pounds but nothing any bigger, although other people were catching bigger ones. Dennis Pye was up and down the Broads and he was catching them, as well as lots of big rudd and tench.

Eight pounds was our best pike that summer, so we decided we would have to return in the winter. Summer piking was almost unheard of: the first frost of October was considered the signal to start pike fishing. In many clubs the rules wouldn't allow fishing any sooner, but if we couldn't wait we used to tackle up for big perch – twenty pound perch! Our tackle was very simple: I used my big star-back wooden reel, which I still take for a day's fishing now and then, remembering old times. I had a split bamboo rod about ten foot long and as stiff as a poker; cuttyhunk lines were the norm, with a Jardine snap tackle, and a big *Fishing Gazette* pike 'bung' fixed to the line. The *Gazette* bung was a big egg-shaped float with a split down the side, and you would stop the float on the line with a wooden peg. Then there were little pilot floats fixed above it, and for these I drilled oak apples and painted them red. When the big pike bung went under the water you could see where it was going by the pilot floats ploughing across the surface. Often I would use two or even three pilot floats, thinking that because I had more pilot floats than the others I was the bees' knees, especially as some of my mates couldn't afford even one.

So that was my first trip to the Broads; but later, when I became mobile, I went up there a lot – with the use of an old Ford Eight, my mate and I would often travel up from Kent in the wintertime. We didn't have car heaters in those days; indicators were little orange 'arms' which shot out left or right when you wanted to signal you were turning; and there were no radios or anything fancy like that, so motoring in winter could be an uncomfortable experience. On these winter trips we used to take our dogs and guns as well, because we would do a bit of wildfowling: the Norfolk Broads were superb for fowling. So there would be me and my mate, two dogs, and all the gear for fishing and fowling for the weekend; and we used to sleep in the car, too! On a very cold night the condensation would ice up, so we would go up to the local tavern, buy a shandy and stay there until we got chucked out; then it was back to the icy cold car. When we were young we could do these things – it was part of the adventure – and would get home on the Sunday night tired and dirty. We didn't shave, but we always had a toothbrush – we felt we could put up with anything as long as our teeth were clean.

The Norfolk Broads have always been a favourite haunt of mine and I still like going back, even though today we don't hear the bittern's boom from deep in the reeds; the Broads of my youth have been ruined by the commercialization of what was once a wilderness paradise for the angler, the naturalist and the wildfowler. Back in the fifties there were just a few sailing boats and barges known as wherries, and by and large those who sailed in them were gentlemen, who tried not to disturb the anglers. However even during our first Broads expedition we had one bitter experience with a speedboat owner – perhaps the first of the 'antis'. Every morning between eight and nine o'clock he would come charging down the River Thurne, and without slowing up would turn abruptly in our swim, ruining the fishing for some considerable time. After three or four of these visits we decided to do something about it: working in the darkness, we fixed the ferry chain so that it was just below the surface. And on cue, at about breakfast time, down came our demon speedboat to ruin our fishing for the day. However, the motor and chain connected in mid-river, there was a horrendous screeching of metal, and the boat drifted to a halt. The chain had proved stronger than the prop. We helped him get his boat ashore and at the same time lowered the chain. He thanked us profusely, and that was the last we saw of him or his speedboat!

Sunrise and sunset on the Broads are often spectacular, and many a morning I have sat entranced with the sun rising and the mist rolling off the water. Silently through the swirling mist a wherry would appear in full sail; on the far bank, a windmill would gradually take form; the bream would begin rolling on the surface; a pike would strike for an early breakfast. Perfect paradise!

FEN TIGER

'Fen Tiger' was the old name given to those who lived in the fens, though the Fen Tiger I knew was far from being a real tiger: he was a small quiet man with glasses, his black hair, thinning a bit on top, combed back and heavily greased. It was said that he used a jar of haircream every other day – perhaps he fancied himself as another Dennis Compton. As a boy in Wisbech where he was born and bred, he was known as 'Muck Sayers', and it seems he was always up to boyish pranks. In the summer he used to live and work on an uncle's farm: he really loved the great outdoors.

During the war, Arthur Sayers served in the Royal Navy as a writer, and spent most of his time in the Far East in charge of Japanese POW working parties. I was introduced to him when he moved to Kent, and our first day of fishing together was at Burham claypit on a July day in 1958. The temperature was well into the eighties, there wasn't a breath of wind, and the water was flat calm and gin clear. It was one of those days when you couldn't have too much to drink and you didn't expect to catch any fish. Arthur tackled up with a 14-foot Spanish reed rod with a split bamboo tip, a centre-pin reel and 2lb line. He fished a float using its bottom ring only, with bread as bait, and he was soon catching nice roach. I was amazed that any fish could be caught under these conditions, and towards the end of the day he also had a couple of tench. From that day on we were always fishing somewhere together, either in salt- or freshwater.

DOUBLE DISASTER

Another thing that Arthur liked to do was to have a flutter on the horses, or if they weren't running, on the dogs. In fact he would have a gamble on anything, even two gentles racing across the top of a tackle box. We had some good fishing times together, Arthur and I, but also some disasters – like the day I lost a record chub. We had gone fishing on the Medway at Teston on one of those lovely autumn days in November that anglers love so much, when the mist lies over the river valleys. As we walked from Teston station we glanced upriver to the weir pool, but then switched our attention back downriver towards Barming. Soon we came to an area with willows on the far bank and, as I stopped to light a cigarette, a roach rolled. I suggested to Arthur that we should fish here as the roach were priming, and so we did. The bank was a bit boggy, but firm enough to put our baskets on.

I tackled up with a 12-foot split bamboo rod, centre-pin reel and 3lb line with a small cork on quill float to take four BB shot. I whipped on a size 12 spade-end hook, plumbed the depth at around eight feet and set the float at ten. My usual way of fishing in those days was 'laying on', with bread flake or crust as bait. Sometimes I would use gentles or, if the water was high and coloured, a big lobworm.

After catching a few nice roach I decided to put out a pike bait, and soon a *Fishing Gazette* bung was floating on the surface with a roach suspended underneath it. For most of the day nothing happened. Then around three o'clock the pike bung started to move around, and would sometimes bob under. I said to Arthur, 'There's a Jack pike around the bait, but he can't take the float under for long. Next time it goes under I'm going to strike.' That's what I did, and I felt a powerful surge as line was taken off the reel.

'Good fish this, Arthur. Could be a double.' Soon I was in control and had the fish coming in. There was a swirl, and the biggest chub I'd seen in my life was on the surface about twelve feet out from the bank. It was huge. It was more than that: it was a record!

I shouted, 'Bring the net, Arthur, bring the net! We've got an enormous fish here – it's a record chub!' He came stumbling up the bank carrying my big landing net. As he arrived I dragged the fish steadily closer to the bank. It was mine; no way could I lose it now. But Arthur, in his haste put the net to the fish instead of sinking the net under the water. The chub struggled; it was hooked by just one point of a treble hook, and the point pulled out. The fish disappeared slowly into the murky water of the River Medway.

I was shattered, and in anger and frustration said to Arthur, 'You bloody idiot! You *know* you don't take a net to a fish; you bring the fish to the net. What did you do that for? I've lost a record chub now!' And I really think I had. My legs trembled and my hands shook as I sat on my basket and lit another cigarette. There were tears in my eyes. I was devastated! . . . But life goes on.

The fishing couldn't go on because it was coming towards dusk, and I said to Arthur, 'That's it! I'm not fishing no more today. We might as well as go home.' It was a long slow trudge up the river bank. The basket weighed heavy on my shoulder as I clutched my rod holdall, and I was still feeling shattered. But that wasn't the end of the story: we got to Maidstone station and, as was usual before we changed trains, I dashed to the other side to get the *London Evening Standard*. Then it was onto the Strood train where we checked Arthur's football coupon: it wasn't a good day for Arthur as he had only three draws. Then I said, 'Hold on a minute, Arthur, I've got my coupon here somewhere. I forgot to give it to George yesterday, but let's check it anyway.' We did, and I had eight draws – twenty four points, the treble chance! The nearest that week was seven. I felt gutted again; it was definitely *not* my day. But Arthur and I were back on the river bank as usual the next day: as I said – life goes on!

Then there was the time of the Christmas roach. We had planned to go fishing at Teston on the day after Boxing Day; it was an annual event. On Christmas Day I went fishing on my own, and when I got back home the usual Christmas party was in progress. The house was a-jumping, with records playing. Dad said, 'Want a drink?'

'No thanks,' I told him. 'I'm going to bed. I've got to be up early for fishing in the morning.'

'Go on,' he said. 'One drink won't hurt.'

I picked up the whisky bottle and swallowed. I continued to drink from the bottle, and then I remembered no more. It wasn't until late on Boxing Day that I returned to the land of living, and I felt terrible. I sorted out my tackle and then went back to bed, really annoyed with myself. The morning came all too quickly. I staggered downstairs, boiled the kettle and, while making my sandwiches, managed to swallow half a cup of strong sweet tea. Then it was out of the house and down to Strood station where Arthur was waiting.

'You all right?' he asked.

'No, mate, I feel terrible. I've been out cold for about twenty-four hours 'cos I drank too much whisky on Christmas night. Didn't even go fishing yesterday.'

We arrived at Teston with me still staggering around and Arthur grabbing hold of me so that I wouldn't tumble in the water. We had intended fishing towards Wateringbury, but we stopped at a small bay above Teston weir. 'This will do me for the day, Arthur; I can't walk any further,' I told him. And that's where I fished, with Arthur just a few yards above me. I tackled up with a 14-foot cane rod, a centre-pin reel and some 3lb line; the float was an old porcupine quill with double rubber rings. I fished laying-on style, with bread flake on a size 10 hook. The water was around eight feet deep, and I introduced some mashed bread as groundbait, cast out and tightened down to the float. Within seconds there was a slight movement and then the float was gone: I struck, and the first fish was on – a lovely roach of over a pound. My day was starting okay, and I felt better already!

The fishing that day was excellent, and every roach was over the pound, the best going 1lb 14oz. I had thirty-two fish, while all those round me struggled for a fish or two; I had certainly hit on a winning swim. On the way home, Arthur said, 'You should drink whisky more often if it means your fishing is going to be that good.'

BARE FACTS

I don't suppose there are many people who have shot a brace of duck while stark naked, but I did. There I stood without a stitch of clothing when two mallard appeared, coming towards me. I quickly grabbed my gun, stuffed two shells in the breech and snapped it shut. I watched the pair of mallard come closer and closer, and soon they were within range. I pulled onto the first duck and fired: it plummeted to earth. Then I was onto the second duck. Swinging through I pulled the trigger, and there was a satisfying thump as 1¼ ounces of size 4 shot was sent skywards. The duck staggered as just one or two shot found their mark. This one was winged, and I watched it glide down onto the water a few hundred yards away where it was lost from sight. Time for Drake to earn his keep. I sent him for the runner; the first duck wasn't going anywhere. Soon he was back with that look on his face that says, 'There you are, boss'. I dispatched the bird and sent Drake off for the other one while I got dressed in very wet and cold clothing. If I was to survive the day I would need plenty of exercise to keep warm.

The day had started off at Otterham Quay, about an hour before dawn on a very cold, frosty morning in November. Arthur, Frank Edmonds and Mick De-La-Mare were going out into the Thames estuary to fish for cod and dabs; on the way they were to drop me off on Berntwick Island where I would spend the day shooting. Everything was fine as we travelled downriver, enjoying bacon sandwiches and scalding mugs of tea. The first glimmer of a false dawn showed, and then the sky turned various shades of pink and blue. Soon we could make out the creeks and small islands, beyond which the flame of the Cat Cracker burned brightly on the Isle of Grain. Curlews called with their lovely bubbling sound as they flitted to and fro, and there was the haunting cry of the oystercatcher, a call that reminds me so much of the northern rivers and moorland in spring.

On the banks of the muddy foreshore sat half a dozen shelduck in their plumage of white, reddish-brown and black, the males with a large red knob on the bill. They are not a sporting duck, but nice to see; at moulting time there would be as many as a hundred at a time on one of the many Medway estuary islands. Then we heard the whistle of the cock widgeon, and the purring sound of the hen. I spotted about thirty widgeon flighting together. Great black-backed gulls were also floating around looking for an easy meal; these gulls are real scavengers. Out on our starboard side we passed a cormorant sitting on a channel marker buoy, reminding me of the vultures in South America. Off to the port side a bunch of teal sprang skywards. The wind was very light, but for ideal shooting conditions I would have preferred a gale. Soon Berntwick Island was in sight; another ten minutes and it would be time for me to leave the others for the day. Frank throttled back the engine, then went into reverse to combat the strong ebbing tide, and continued to juggle with the controls. Mick was up in the pulpit with a boat-hook, shouting out the depth of water.

'We won't be able to stop because we're on a falling tide,' Frank said as he went in as close to the island as he dared. First the dog was sent over the side and was soon swimming for the shore; then as we came close in, I dropped the gun, bag and decoys off onto the island. Next it was my turn. I told Arthur 'Catch a few dabs for me and I'll get you a brace of duck.'

Mick called out, 'Ten feet . . . six feet . . .' Then a pause and, 'Two feet . . . Jump!' And I did; into about twelve feet of icy cold water, and sank like a stone. After the initial shock my instinct for survival took over and I swam for the surface; but as I did, I could hear the propeller turning above my head so moved as far away as possible before popping up. Gasping in air and spitting out water at the same time, I tried to crawl up the muddy bank but it was hard going and I kept slipping back. Once again my will to survive drove me on; that same instinct has got me out of a lot of trouble over the years. I pulled out my big Bowie knife and stuck it into the muddy bank for leverage, and only then was I able to drag myself to safety. Finally I lay exhausted on the scrub grass.

Arthur called, 'You all right, boy?'

'Yeah,' I said through chattering teeth as I put my legs in the air and emptied the water out of my waders.

'See you at five o'clock,' Arthur shouted. Then *Teal*, with Frank at the wheel, headed off after the cod and dabs of the Thames estuary while I stripped off to wring some of the water from my clothes. There I was, naked as the day I was born, when those two mallard appeared over the horizon.

Drake and I spent the morning creek-crawling through some of the most glutinous black mud to be found anywhere in the country. At lunchtime we crawled out onto the spartina grass and lay there catching our breath. We were both tired, but after a break we headed off to an old concrete block-house, Drake to have a drink of fresh water and a sleep; me to have some hot soup and a smoke. But disaster had struck a second time: when I went for my early morning swim, the matches were in my jacket pocket. Now, of course, I discovered they were a soggy mess.

No soup, tea or a smoke: how would I survive the day? I had brought with me a Primus stove, some bread, soup and the tea-making things, but with no way of lighting the Primus most of this was useless. I was starving, so it was dry bread and cold vegetable soup: ghastly! And soon Drake and I were back to creek-crawling, if only to try and forget the hunger pains and to keep warm. The bigger problem for me at that time was not being able to have a cigarette or a pipe of tobacco. Thankfully for many years now I've not smoked, and packing up the smoking habit was one of the best things I ever did.

So we spent the afternoon creek-crawling until the flooding tide forced us onto the firmer ground of the marsh, among the bladder wrack and spartina grass. Then it became dark, but there was no sign of *Teal* and my three friends. The tide was making fast, so Drake and I moved to an old wreck. The water had now reached Drake's tummy, and things were starting to look serious. Soon I had to pick Drake up and hang him around my neck. The water rose above my knees and, as it reached the short and curly parts, I gave a gasp. I was wet, cold and hungry, and very worried.

The water had just reached my waist when *Teal* appeared some four-hundred yards offshore in the darkness. Mick was up in the pulpit, boat-hook at the ready; Arthur was in the stern. Then we were safe. I handed Arthur my dog, and then the gun and the ducks, and I swung over the side. He gave me a cup of hot soup. With my bag of six mallard, three teal and a widgeon, we headed off for Otterham quay, a hot bath and some dry clothes. What a day it had been!

People ask why I did it. I reply, because it was fun and I enjoyed it immensely, despite the odd moments of danger; though it was probably no more risky than driving round the M25 today.

BIG CHUB

Some thirty years later the Fen Tiger was with me when I caught a magnificent brace of chub on the last day of the season. I had driven down from my home in Lancashire's Ribble Valley to spend the last day of the season fishing with Arthur. Over supper that night we discussed where to go for the last day.

'What about Swanton Morley on the Wensum?' I suggested. Arthur agreed, and the next morning we struggled down to the river with all our tackle. I picked a straight stretch below a bend where the water was about four feet deep. About five yards below my chosen swim was a small bay, but at first I ignored this fishy spot. Chub were far from my mind, and it was the Wensum roach I had come to catch. I tackled up with a light quivertip rod, a thirty-year-old Mitchell 300 reel, a paternoster rig and a size 22 hook baited with a bronze gentle. The main line was 1½lb b.s., and the hook length just 1lb. In the next four hours I had six bites: I missed three and was broken by three fish.

I suspected chub. At midday the bailiff came along for a chat and to check our permits, and he mentioned there were some good chub to about four pounds. At this news I tackled up another quivertip rod with 4lb line, a link ledger carrying three swan shot, and a number 8 hook. My bait was a large piece of bread flake smeared with cheese spread which I cast across and downstream about fifteen yards. Within minutes I had a three-pound chub in the net. I rebaited and cast to the same spot. Soon I was into a really good fish which put up a super scrap, thumping hard all the way to the net. It was a perfect chub. I trembled as I zeroed the scales with the weigh net: the fish weighed 5lb 7oz. I left it in the landing net to recover before I took some pictures of it.

'What a way to end the season!' I thought. I flopped into my chair and said to Arthur, 'I think I'll sleep for the rest of the day'. Then, as an afterthought, I added, 'If I'd caught a six-pounder I'd have done a streak across the river.' I relaxed, thinking about the pictures we would be able to take of the fish a little later. But after a rest I decided to have another go, and I baited once more with bread flake smeared with cheese spread. Within ten minutes the rod tip pulled round and my answering strike saw it pulled savagely down to the surface. Line flew from the spool, sounding like a scalded cat, and for a while it was a battle with neither side winning. Then the fish swirled on the surface and soon I was easing it over the landing net. It was mine. Adrenalin was pumping through my body as I realized that I might have managed a brace of five-pound chub in a single session. Out came the scales again, only this time they bumped down to 6lb 2oz.

We rounded up witnesses, weighed both 'fish a couple of times, and then took some pictures. The chub were returned to the river, hopefully to grow into seven-pounders. I felt the water and decided that streaking was out of the question. Perhaps when I catch a seven-pounder . . .

Two weeks later the weights and measures inspector in Blackburn told me the scales were weighing two ounces under, but I was more than happy to leave the weight at 6lb 2oz for my best chub to date.

IRISH ADVENTURES

The Emerald Isle has always been a magnet for those keen on shooting and fishing, and I've had some super times there with my friends and with my son Nigel. My first trip to Ireland was to shoot snipe and duck with John Williams, a fanatical wildfowler from Nottingham who often travelled down to shoot the North Kent marshes in winter.

John and I arrived at Manchester Airport on a cold autumn day, overcast with squally showers: perfect conditions for a duck-shooting holiday. We were off to County Cavan in Southern Ireland, taking an Aer Lingus flight to Dublin. As we circled the bay before landing the sun was shining in a clear blue sky and only a light westerly wind ruffled the waters: the weather had turned against us! What we really wanted was what Ireland is famous for: gale force winds and heavy rain; but I guess only wildfowlers would understand this.

Within two hours we were sitting in the bar of the Derragarra Inn at Butler's Bridge on the banks of the River Annalee not very far from Cavan town, sampling the Irish hospitality. For John it was a Guinness; for me an orange juice (I was the driver for that part of the trip!). Cavan is a large town by Irish standards, with some 5,000 people; it has a lovely old church and some nice shops, and we found the girls very friendly too – many a drinking session lasted well into the small hours of the morning, with just a couple of hours sleep before we were out for the dawn flight.

One particular dawn springs to mind. A certain Michael and Seamus had promised us some excellent duck shooting and were to take us out on one of the lakes; this meant a boat trip in the darkness so that we could arrive at the hides before first light and get the decoys out on the water. To say that we – four adults with no life jackets, two dogs and a sack of decoys in a 14-foot dinghy – had a hair-raising trip across the lake in the dark with a force 6 to 8 westerly blowing is an understatement. And all for a duck or two: the daft things we do when we are young!

We sped through one lake and towards another by way of a narrow, twisting stream which seemed to be flowing at a fair rate of knots. Bushes and reedbeds appeared out of the darkness, sometimes catching us across the face and hands. I was just thinking, 'What on earth am I doing in this watery hell with two crazy Irish characters?' when the boat shuddered to a grinding halt. We had run aground on rocks. In fact half an hour later, as the sky began to lighten, we saw that we were in just a foot of water with some 800 yards still to go to reach the other lake and the duck hides. After a few mouthfuls of whiskey we went over the side and up to our knees in ice-cold water and, with much heaving and swearing, moved the boat into deeper water. The shear-pin on the motor had gone, but thankfully Seamus had a spare and soon we were on our way – and just as fast as before, despite John and I urging that we should take things easy.

Daylight was with us now, and John and I were fed up. John said, 'Sod the ducks, let's go back for a hot bath and some breakfast,' and it did sound tempting. But in for a penny, in for a pound, that's me, and I convinced John that we should carry on; after all, it had already cost us a small fortune in whiskey. We left the narrow channel and entered a vast expanse of windswept water, angry with white horses. The bows dug deep in the waves and there was no way we were going to cross the lake to get to the hides on the opposite shoreline.

Then the motor died.

We were at the mercy of the wind and waves, and were being pushed back into the mouth of the stream; though at least there we would be in shallow water, with little chance of drowning. While Seamus and Michael refilled the fuel tank, John and I decided that we had to end our relationship with these two characters, so we asked them to take us back, promising them a bottle of whiskey. We had had quite enough of duck shooting for one day. And so five hours after leaving the guest house we returned for a hot bath and a late breakfast; even the poor old dogs seemed fed up with boat trips, and more than pleased to be back on terra firma. We spent the rest of the day walking around the lakeside and ditches in the hope of surprising a duck or two, and the dogs enjoyed the exercise. We had a few shots: John bagged three mallard and two pigeons, and I had two rabbits and a mallard.

I have also spent lots of holidays in Ireland with another John, John Bodsworth, shooting and fishing north and south of the border, and we have had some great times. I first met John when I was planning a trip to Ireland in the 1970s. On that occasion I intended fishing with Cormack Walsh on his MV *Kingfisher* out of Dungarvan in County Waterford, and the quarry were to be conger eel, pollack, ling and blue shark. Cormack and I had enjoyed excellent sport in the past, fishing with light tackle for pollack over wrecks, with sand-eels as our bait. On one trip we invited three English anglers to join us, and the five of us landed over 750 pounds of fish in a day; all except one were returned to the sea. That was the kind of fishing you could expect in Ireland.

John Bodsworth was an all-action man. Back in the 1960s he had played lead guitar in a rock group, then he had built up a successful building business, and all the while spending a fair part of his time enjoying rough shooting, as well as sea, coarse and game fishing. He also knew Ireland well; indeed, long before we met he had fished all around the coast, and he had also done quite a lot of coarse fishing. John and I hit it off the minute we met, and over the years we have been able to help one another catch some good fish in both salt- and freshwater. Right from the start we had much in common: we had both travelled a lot in Europe and South America, and above all we both have a zest for life. Even at sixty plus John is still doing all the things he did all those years ago (except he no longer plays lead guitar!).

On our first Irish adventure we had with us Arthur Sayers (the Fen Tiger) and John Pilkington, a chemist from Lancashire; it was their first visit, and unfortunately the week was a disaster as regards the fishing. The weather was foul, we were shore-bound for most of the time, and there were no dinghies available for fishing the estuary for flounders and bass. We did fish the Black-water estuary from the shore, catching small conger on light tackle that was more suited to pike fishing, and this proved quite good fun. But with just two half-days afloat at the end of our holiday all we had caught were a few small conger, ling and pollack; but we had had plenty of laughs.

In the early 1980s my son Nigel, John Bodsworth and I hired a Shannon cruiser in order to go up the Shannon into Lough Ree to fish for bream, rudd, and pike; we also hoped to fit in some duck shooting. Lough Ree is some seventeen miles long and runs from Lansborough in the north to Athlone in the south. It is dotted with islands and has hundreds of reedy, intimate bays – a paradise for anglers, wildfowlers and the naturalist.

The trip went well. By the end of the first week we had caught lots of fish, including specimen bream for both John and me, for which we won Irish Spe-cimen Fish badges and certificates. We also had plenty of laughs, such as the time I met up with a couple of local girls who worked at one of the inns. I was between marriages and invited them back to the cruiser after they finished work the following evening. John, Nigel and I sat in the cabin drinking wine and wondering if the two local beauties would turn up, when we heard a car. Nigel shot up from the table and disappeared into his cabin, to reappear soon after dressed in all his latest gear and smelling of my Aramis aftershave. After a quick preen before the mirror, Nigel bounded across the gangway and up to the car that had just parked. What a shock he had: it wasn't the two bar-maids, but a courting couple. Talk about egg on his face!

During this trip we met a couple of German anglers who were staying at a nearby guesthouse. One time when John and I returned from shooting rabbits, their landlady invited us in for a drink, and a bottle of Schnapps was pro-duced: my favourite tipple! One drink led to another, and another, and before I knew what was happening I was legless and extremely merry, to say the least. Somehow John got me back in the car in time for dinner – and of course that meant another couple of glasses of wine. It took me most of the next day to return to the land of the living, and the fishing; but the shooting had to take a back seat for a couple of days: drink and guns do not mix, and I was a bit groggy for quite a while.

MAGIC MOMENT

We found a good mooring spot on Lough Ree at Barrymore. There the bream fishing was excellent, with many fish over 7lb and a few breaking the 8lb barrier. But the most amazing thing about this area was the rudd, which were not residents: a shoal would appear from nowhere about every four or five days. We were there at one such magic moment. It was a perfect September evening and we were up on deck sharing a bottle of wine after a very good dinner cooked by John. The sun was a huge ball of fire slowly disappearing over the horizon, and the water was flat calm. Then suddenly the mirror-like surface was broken by the dorsal fins of dozens of big rudd. They were everywhere, swirling and turning for the mass of flies lying dead or dying on the surface. It was an incredible sight.

We forgot about the wine and made a mad dash for the tackle. We set the floats at two feet, with the shot bunched directly underneath them so that our pieces of bread flake would float on the surface; it was a winning method. In the fading light we had to squint to see our floats, but the fish were ready to take our baits directly they hit the water, and soon all three of us were playing large rudd. We were having a ball, and we whooped for joy as hard-fighting rudd dived for the bottom in fifteen feet of water. Many of the fish were over two pounds.

The excitement ended as quickly as it had begun: after an hour and a half the fish had disappeared and it was back to the wine, discussing the wonderful sport we had enjoyed in the setting sun on an Irish lough.

One fish that I shall never forget was a pike I caught from a backwater on the River Shannon. I was staying at Athlone in one of the many guesthouses that cater for visiting anglers, and this time the weather was terrible. Day after day the sky was leaden, the rain sheeted down, rivers burst their banks, lakes became coloured and flooded the surrounding land. It was a case of looking for pastures new, and I chose Murray's Bar, a fabulous place with no carpets on the stone floor, where you will find the best of traditional music, a few miles outside the town of Athlone, near the mouth of the River Inny. On this particular night there was live music and the place was packed with young and old, locals and visitors, all having a good time. I was sitting glass in hand listening to the music and eyeing up the local talent when a voice said, 'Are you Martin James? PJ told me you would be here.' (Peter, known to his friends as PJ, was a super chap.)

'That's me, mate,' I said. 'Wanna drink?'

He introduced himself as John Murphy, and asked if I had caught many fish, so I told him about the flooded rivers and lakes. He then told me about a bay down at Shannon Bridge near the power station, which in flood conditions was said to be very good for tench and bream. I thanked him and we sat drinking and chatting about all manner of things from the price of petrol to politicians; in fact we put the world to rights. When the music ended most of the patrons moved off for home, some a little worse for drink, but a select few, including John and me, moved into the back room for a mug of tea and a bite to eat with Mary and her mother, a lovely couple. Some time around two in the morning I headed for home.

Next day, after a huge breakfast (all Irish breakfasts are huge) I loaded the tackle into the car and headed for the flooded bay near Shannon Bridge power station. I arrived to find the river the colour of pea-green soup, and rafts of rubbish being carried seawards. A large tree trunk crashed into a bridge support and spun away on the still rising river, and conditions were undoubtedly far from perfect, to say the least. However, much of the surface of the bay was covered with waterlilies which to my mind made it a very pikey-looking area, so I decided to fish 'sink and draw' with a dead roach bait. I tackled up with a 12-foot glass carp rod, an old Mitchell reel of 1953 vintage, 10lb line and 15 inches of wire trace with a couple of size 8 treble hooks. Having baited up, I cast towards the far bank and waited for the bait to sink to the bottom in about twelve feet of water; then I made a series of short retrieves. On the second cast I had a pike of about 5lb, and two casts later I was into another fish of the same size: good sport under the conditions.

I baited with a fresh roach and made a cast towards the far bank, watching the line sink slowly as the bait drifted to the bottom. I began my series of retrieves, and on the fourth retrieve tried to lift the bait off the bottom – but nothing moved. 'Damn it!' I said out loud, thinking that my hooks had got stuck in the lilies. I pulled, but still nothing gave. I relaxed the pressure, and then the line began moving very slowly away to my right: a fish had picked up the bait and was heading towards the mouth of the bay and the fast-flowing river.

I made a powerful strike, and the reel screamed as a fish took line. 'This feels like a good double,' I thought. 'It might go about fifteen pounds if I'm lucky!' My unseen adversary shot out of the quiet lily-covered bay into the raging River Shannon and, as the current hit it, the rod tip stabbed down to the surface and more line was torn from the reel. This *was* a good fish! I tried to take in some line, but without success; it was a case of hang on and hope it would tire. With the rod bent double, the reel grudgingly gave a few more feet of line, and then without warning the fish kited into the quieter water beside the bank. I wound down and pumped the fish towards me, gaining line all the time. It was tiring, or so I thought.

Suddenly the fish seemed to gain renewed energy: it moved out into the current, and the reel howled in protest as it took all the line I had worked so hard to retrieve. A real battle royal was taking place in the depths of the flooded Shannon. Again I began to pump the fish towards me, and foot by foot I was getting line back on the reel and the fish towards the waiting landing net. I wondered if it was well hooked, and whether the hooks would hold. For at least fifteen minutes I didn't see it, and then suddenly it swirled on the surface. It was huge! It swirled again, shook its head and dived for the depths. I eased off the pressure: this was a good fish, and I was desperate to land it though by now my hands were shaking.

The fish made one last effort to rid itself of this thing that kept dragging it towards the surface, but the hooks held firm and I began gaining line more quickly. I was very much aware that such a big fish could have something left for another bid for freedom; but suddenly it was on the surface, thrashing, twisting and shaking its head in its effort to get rid of the hooks which I could see were firmly fixed in the scissors. I stepped back and dragged it over the waiting net which a passer-by held for me. The pike was mine, and I could see it was a twenty-pounder, a truly magnificent fish.

I was shaking with excitement – or was it the fear that I might lose the fish at the last moment? It doesn't matter how many big fish we catch, it's the same feeling every time, and the day that feeling leaves me will be the day I put my rods away; but I hope it never comes as long as I can draw my breath!

Out with the scales and the big weigh-net: this was the moment of truth. The needle moved round, past 10 . . . 20 . . . 25 . . . and came to rest at 26lb 6oz: a personal-best river pike, taken on a day when conditions looked hopeless. I shot a whole roll of film of that special fish, and then released it, hoping it would grow into a thirty-pounder.

What a day, and it still wasn't lunchtime! But the pubs would be open, and it was time to celebrate. I went up to Killeen's Bar, and as usual Derry Killeen was pulling pints of Guinness. After recounting the capture of my fish I celebrated with a glass of cognac and a bacon sandwich. You will find a picture of that fish in the bar, should you be passing, and in Murray's Bar, too, where I spent that night celebrating its capture.

AMBUSH

Mind you, that certainly wasn't the biggest pike I encountered in Ireland; I hooked a much bigger one when John Bodsworth and I were fishing in County Cavan. We had gone across in John's converted van, which was like home from home. One day we were sitting at the waterside when from nowhere appeared this bedraggled figure, his threadbare herring-bone coat tied up with string, and string through his boots.

'Ah,' he said, 'You'll be fishin' for pike.'

I nodded, and he sat down with us. I always had a bottle of whiskey in the basket for these occasions, and I poured a large tumbler of the amber liquid for our newfound friend. One glass followed another and soon he was quite legless, but he chatted away, telling us of a lake where the pike were as big as crocodiles. After discovering from him the location of this lake we sent him on his way, although not in a straight line.

John said, 'Shall we look at this pike lake the leprechaun was on about?'

I agreed we should, and we drove around until eventually we found the iron gates that led to the estate lake we were looking for. Everything was just as the old man had described it. We parked the van, clambered through a hole in the fence and made our way along a narrow track which ran down to the lakeside. The lake covered some six acres and was surrounded by trees and shrubs, with two-thirds of the water covered by waterlilies. Great swathes of reed grew at the water's edge; coots and moorhens sailed across the glass-like surface; pigeons cooed in the trees; small fish dimpled the lake surface.

Then the mosquitoes hit us: they had surely been waiting in ambush. Suddenly, with no warning, they dived for our exposed skin, biting and drawing blood: I thought for a moment that I was back in the Amazon jungle. These mosquitoes were in a foul mood and determined to devour us – as we killed one, another ten took its place. Was our Irish leprechaun wreaking his vengeance on us for getting him so drunk, or were the mosquitoes defending these so-called giant pike from anglers? We beat a retreat back to the van to lick our wounds. John brewed tea and made some sandwiches, and we talked about this lovely water guarded by its army of insects. However, we decided to fish it despite the flying, stinging, biting guardians.

Next morning after breakfast we made our way to the water's edge, tackled up with two rods apiece, one for catching bait, the other for the pike. We chose a gap in the reeds and threw in a handful of gentles, and the water boiled with rudd competing for the free offerings. John baited a size 16 hook with two gentles and cast out; the next instant he was swinging in a rudd of about six ounces and dropping it into the landing net. Soon he had a dozen or so to use as bait. It was my turn now, so I baited with a freshly killed rudd, set the float at six feet and cast out. Then I went back to the urgent task of killing mosquitoes.

It was probably an hour later that the float began moving slowly across the surface. I picked up the rod, tightened down to the fish and struck hard. The leprechaun had been right: this was a big one, and I was lucky that it shot out towards the centre of the lake and not into the margins where it could so easily have broken me on one of the many snags.

For some time the fight was fairly evenly balanced: the fish would take a bit of line and then I would get some back. This seesaw battle lasted about ten minutes, but I was gradually gaining line. Then when the pike was about five yards from the bank I spotted it: it was a monster, the biggest freshwater fish I had ever seen on the end of a line in the British Isles.

We both gasped. I said, 'Bloody hell! Get the net, Jimbo.'

Then the pike decided to go skywards, coming out of the water tail-walking, head-shaking. It was a magnificent fish. We could see its every detail: it was awesome. I put it at between thirty-five and forty pounds, and it was on the end of my line!

Then disaster: the line went slack, and the fish was gone. The swivel had broken. I was devastated, because no way did I ever think I would lose that fish.

I sat down, despondent. The mosquitoes didn't matter any more. 'Did you see the size of that, Jimbo?' I was shaking and shattered. I had lost the fish of a lifetime. Even as I write these words I can still feel the bites of the mosquitoes and see that pike going skywards shaking its head and flaring its gills. Yes, a certain lake in Ireland owes me a big fish. One day I hope to go back there with John.

CHAPTER 5

Further Afield

A Poem About Litter

The weeping willow sheds real tears;
Man has answered all her fears.
The carpet at her feet so green
Now presents a tragic scene,
Strewn with litter, bottles, cans
Tossed aside by thoughtless hands.
Broken glass glints in the sun,
Wildlife can no longer run
In safety by the riverside,
Or find a sheltered place to hide.
The water chokes upon its way,
With banks in total disarray.
Among the weeds, a broken line,
A bird that can no longer fly.
Can man so hurt the countryside?
Has he lost his sense of pride
In all the beauty waiting there
That Nature gives for us to share?
And with the willow fall my tears,
But I will try to solve her fears
And take away the waste thrown down,
To leave but footprints on the ground.
And will you help to ease her pain.
And make Mother Nature smile again?

Lorraine Davies

As a writer and broadcaster I wanted to bring my readers and listeners tales from interesting places around the world. One such place was South America. I had been intrigued by this huge continent since I was a youngster reading the *Boys' Own* magazine and my history books about the Spanish conquests of this part of the world. Above all I had been inspired by stories of the Amazon jungle and the famed Amazon woman in one of the Tarzan films.

I have been very fortunate in spending a considerable amount of time in Peru, Colombia, Brazil and Venezuela as writer, photographer, traveller and angler. It was a most fascinating experience, especially when I left the towns and villages and travelled along the rivers or into the jungle. This was a different world, and at times a very inhospitable one. In the jungle I came across snakes of all sizes, including the giant anaconda, and there were also dangerous spiders and ants; however, most of the animals and birds were quite harmless. In fact, and contrary to what we had been told, they usually moved away from us as we hacked our way through the jungle. We had been led to expect attacks by ferocious animals such as the jaguar or the cayman, a South American alligator, but we never even saw a jaguar. The biggest and most savage ceature we had to contend with was *homo sapiens*: he was a savage, a killer and a thief, and you could never trust him.

We saw macaws, parakeets, herons, egrets, toucans and many other birds of quite magnificent colours, several of species that I couldn't identify. Whenever I saw a toucan I thought of a cooling glass of Guinness and imagined that I was sitting in an Irish bar, far away from the stinking villages that we often visited in our South American travels.

Most of the jungle towns were simply groups of hovels smelling of excrement, dead dogs, rotten fruit and fish. Don't ever talk to me about poverty: in the United Kingdom we don't know what it is. You have to go to Third World countries to see real poverty. In Bogota, for example, children live in sewers and old ladies in concrete storm pipes. On the outskirts of big towns like Leticia the filth was ever-present, as was the problem of exhaust fumes.

Howler monkeys were everywhere, and we had many a meal of monkey and rice, though I found this meat rather stringy. We often had snake meat, which was quite good if a bit tough; and a quite excellent meal was pineapple, papayas, bananas and rice with snake or catfish. Finally alligator was one of my favourite meats, far better than the more generally available cow or donkey.

Crossing the rivers was a major problem, especially when you had to wade the shallow stretches, because the most dangerous creature of all, both in my opinion and in that of many other experienced travellers in this region, was a tiny minnow-like fish known as the *candiru*, far more deadly than a piranha or a water snake. If a candiru gets inside you it can eat your guts out, and according to local Indians it can even swim up a stream of urine. Another nasty of the rivers is the stingray, which lies under the sand ready to strike at the unsuspecting traveller.

On the other hand, although a lot is spoken about the cayman or alligator, these were no threat to us: when we approached them they invariably slid off the bank and moved away. But the animals that really grabbed my attention were the pink dolphins. These are big, about the size of a beluga whale and, when they rose up alongside our dugout canoes and crashed back, they rocked us about dangerously. In fact the pink dolphin is now in danger of being wiped out in the Amazon.

One hazard that we and all other river-users faced was attack from bandits. They would appear from nowhere, heavily armed, and it could be a bit scary, especially when the guns were actually being used.

The three main problems out in the field were the mosquitoes, which attacked every bit of exposed flesh; the bushmaster, the largest poisonous snake in the world and one which captures its prey by ambush tactics; and being robbed and killed by cocaine smugglers and terrorists. In Peru, the Shining Path was a particularly vicious guerrilla group that was just coming to prominence, who could butcher you alive and smile at the same time.

I had a very narrow escape one morning. Just after dawn I stepped out of a thicket onto a track no more than eighteen inches wide and came face to face with a dreaded bushmaster, coiled and ready to strike. I froze. I was *extremely* frightened, and that is an understatement. I felt the blood drain from my body. Was I going to die in this steamy, stinking, hellhole of a country? Would it all end here? Then without a sound my friend Ted, a giant of a man from Utah, appeared in front of me and blasted the bushmaster to pieces with his sawn-off pump-action shotgun. You can keep all your automatic weapons and pistols: in the jungle one weapon reigns supreme – the 12-gauge pump-action shotgun, cut down for ease of use.

Colombia and Peru were the countries where cocaine smuggling seemed to be at its worst. But they also had some wonderful fishing in the Rivers Amazon, the Cayaru which flowed inky black through Peru, the Yavary, and in the many huge jungle lakes. The European rivers hold around 150 species of fish, but I'm told that the Amazon system has 1,800 species. Just think: some of the tiny fishes we keep in aquariums at home can grow to a foot long or more in the River Amazon.

LIFE IN LETICIA

Colombia has one, and only one, tiny port on the Amazon: Leticia, two thousand miles from the Atlantic coast and 312 feet above sea level. There, the river is over two miles wide, and when it floods the water can rise forty feet. Its only apparent claim to fame was as a smuggling centre for all kinds of goods, from cocaine to rare animals; it also boasted several brothels, all staffed by girls flown in from Bogota.

One afternoon I flew in from Bogota in an old Dakota with Ted (the bushmaster killer); Rick, a short blond-haired lad from Texas; Warren, a New Yorker; and Jordon, a bear of a man who smoked cigars continuously and who came from Iowa. After clearing customs and paying the usual bribe, we collected our truck from alongside the grass airstrip and headed into town. As we did so, we passed several banners announcing the opening of a new brothel. That's the sort of town Leticia was.

The town was surrounded on three sides by jungle and on the fourth by the mighty Amazon. The place was full of people, and shops selling everything the human race desired: dresses from France, silks from China, shoes from Italy, cameras from Japan. Whisky could be had then, providing you had American dollars. The only ways in and out were by air and by boat. The locals had nowhere to go, and so they used to spend their time driving round and round the square blowing their horns. As a Letician, it seemed that as soon as you made your first few bucks you bought yourself a Japanese motorbike. Later, when you had made a lot more dollars, you bought a car. But there was still nowhere to go until you had made enough to buy a home in Bogota, preferably in the colonial district.

Down on the waterfront, Indian dugouts were tied up beside modern fibreglass boats fitted with the latest Johnson, Evinrude and Mercury outboard motors; there were even outboards fitted on the sterns of dugouts used by the Indians. Often we went by float plane which was perfect for our needs, and both Ted and Jordon were top-class fliers. Sometimes I took the controls, and even brought the plane down on the lakes when the conditions were good. The float plane was ideal for us, because we often visited as many as three countries in a day.

A couple of miles away from Leticia, over the border, was the Brazilian town of Tabatinga. The town was run by the military, and often we would have drinks with the commandant who was in the air force. Tabatinga was just a small Amazonian jungle town, quite different from Leticia, but you still had to pay the usual bribes in American dollars.

DORADO CATFISH

On my trips it was often possible to fish. One such day started around dawn, when my Indian boatman, Ramon, picked me up at the dock; we were to fish the River Cayaru in Peru, and there I hoped to meet some of my Ticuna Indian friends who acted as guides. We moved off with me sitting in the bows tackling up with a 7-foot spinning rod, a multiplier reel and 12lb line. I fixed on a wire trace and a small spinner.

Some thirty minutes after leaving the dock we stopped the boat and I began spinning. Soon the piranhas were coming thick and fast, but I soon tired of this and we moved off to the mouth of the Cayaru to fish for the Dorado catfish, which grow very big. The mosquitoes were trying to eat me alive, but the fishing was more important and so I had to let them feed undisturbed.

For these big catfish I used my 9-foot glass rod, a Penn multiplier reel, a 20lb line and a thick wire trace with two size 5/0 hooks. Bait was supplied by my Indian guide, and consisted of a one pound hunk of fish. The whole lot was thrown over the side and line paid out; then we sat back sharing a coke and watching the odd cayman moving around.

To my left a tree overhung the water, and there I spotted an Indian lad no more than five years of age. He was armed with a spear, and I asked Ramon what the boy was doing.

'Fishing,' Ramon replied. 'He will have to learn to hunt if he is to survive.'

In the next four hours the boy struck twice with the spear, catching a fish each time. He would grow into a good warrior and provider for his family.

Line began to trickle from the reel, click, click, click, then to gather pace and spill more rapidly from the reel. Time for action! Ramon looked at me and said, 'Big fish for Mr Marteen'. I nodded. Down in the dark, deep water something had taken my bait, so I picked up the rod and snapped the reel into gear. The rod slammed down hard, and banged on the side of the boat. Was it a fish or a cayman that had picked up the bait? Line was still streaming from the reel; the check screamed in protest, and the fight was on.

For about half an hour the fish moved up and down the river with Ramon following, and then a huge freshwater dolphin leapt out of the water. I crammed on the pressure, but still the battle raged up and down the Cayaru and it was another thirty minutes before I began to get some control over this powerful underwater force, and could start to pump the fish towards me. As I fought it, Ramon moved the canoe slowly towards the bank; twenty yards downstream the fish rolled on the surface, thrashing the water to a foam. I had never experienced anything like this. Although slowly, I was winning the battle. Even the little Indian boy had stopped his fishing to watch.

We bumped the bank, and the dugout was made firm so that I could get ashore; I planned to finish the fight from a solid platform. Ramon was at my side with an evil-looking gaff attached to a five-foot bamboo pole; not only was it well pointed, but it had barbs up each side. I continued to pump. The fish was tiring fast, and soon it was within reach of Ramon, who didn't waste a second – I dragged it up the bank, flipping, twisting and turning in its bid for freedom, but it had no chance once Ramon had set the gaff. The fish was mine. What a fight these Dorado catfish give, quite different from trout or carp.

We returned to the young lad's village and presented the fish to the villagers, who made us most welcome. The sun burned down with a vengeance so we sat swinging in hammocks, drinking foul-tasting coffee laced with Jack Daniels. Later we dined on the catfish. I was offered the usual reward of a woman for the night, but declined as we had to be ready for another job in the morning. Thus as dusk settled over the Amazon, Ramon gunned the motor and we headed away from the Ticuna Indians to our own camp and some decent coffee. It was the usual hair-raising trip in the pitch black of night, always with the risk of running into bandits or, even worse, drifting tree trunks that could so easily wreck our boat. But we arrived without mishap.

The jungle, the rivers and lakes were a great source of fun. Although I've had a lot of scary moments there, given the chance I would certainly pay a return visit.

FLORIDA BASS AND DOUGHNUTS

For over thirty years I had corresponded with newspaper editor Horace Carter, one of the most experienced Florida anglers, as happy catching the blue gills (a small perch-like fish) as fishing in the sea for big game fish. When we met we found we had a great deal in common; it is like a true brotherhood, this angling business, and he told me lots of stories and showed me many different ways of catching fish. Horace is also an award-winning writer. His book, *Virus of Fear* is a documentary of the day-by-day crusade he waged against the dreaded Klu Klux Klan in the Carolinas from 1949 to 1953. For this he won the prestigious Pulitzer Prize for Meritorious Public Service.

I also met Lakeland tackle dealer Allan Smith, a six-foot guy with bright blue eyes that twinkled whenever he talked about his favourite fish, the bass. Allan would call me up at night and say, 'Wanna go bassing at dawn, Martin?' My answer was always 'Yes, please!' An hour before dawn, with the sound of crickets ringing in our ears, we would be off, stopping at a gas station to collect a bag of ice, some fresh coffee and doughnuts. The latter could often be purchased with a dozen or so different fillings, and my favourite was blueberry: an excellent start to the day.

Arriving at the waterside, I would transfer to the boat and Allan would back the trailer into the water, climb aboard and drive the boat off the trailer. Then it was off, more often than not motoring across a glass-like surface, leaving a creamy trail behind us. As we neared one of Allan's favourite marks the gas guzzler would be killed and a small electric motor switched on, as well as the temperature gauge and the fish and depth finders.

I recall one day when Allan fished for bass with spinner baits and plugs, while I chose a fly-fishing outfit with a very big streamer fly on a size 3/0 hook. The sun was warming us and the water, and ospreys were starting to work the thermals. In Florida the osprey is a common bird, often seen nesting on telegraph poles. Now and again we saw an eagle. We fished in a dozen spots this particular morning but without success; the bass didn't want flies, plugs or shinners (a small chub-like fish that was used as livebait). However, our next trip was a different story. This time we were joined by Dave Carbonie whose job was selling fishing tackle, and the chosen venue was a state-controlled fishery where for the price of a few dollars you could have hundreds of acres of water to fish.

At 8 a.m., with the temperature slowly climbing to the nineties, we launched the boat and motored off. Would the fish be at home? We fished with float tackle and shinners, setting the bait to swim at six feet in some twelve feet of water. Then we sat back; all was lovely. I grabbed a can of ice-cold coke from the ice-box, and Allan and Dave followed suit. But almost immediately Allan's bait was away; a short fight followed and a nice bass was landed. Next it was Dave's turn, and he caught four more bass in quick succession.

My float submerged slowly. I struck, and there was a heavy weight on the end of the line: the grandfather of all bass was moving steadily towards tree roots. I would show these Americans what fishing was all about, I thought smugly. Then the line went slack, and I wound in to find the bait chopped in half. Allan told me the culprit was a turtle, and that they often grabbed the bait before the bass.

We fished on until midday, catching a few more hard-fighting bass to around five pounds; and then, with the temperatures in the nineties, we headed for home and a cold shower. It had been a good morning, and with Kate, my wife of a few weeks, I would be off water-skiing after lunch. What a lovely place Florida can be; it's certainly fun in the sun.

All the people I met in Florida were great, from the girls at Hooters' dressed in short shorts, to the millionaires I fished with out in the Gulf of Mexico. One of the top bass anglers was a guy called Ronnie Waggers. With his partner Dave Hoy, Ronnie runs the Professional Bass Guide Service, especially set up for TV companies who want to make fishing programmes and for out-of-state anglers on vacation. They also offer trips for the businessman who wants to impress an important client. In the UK it is the golf course; in Florida it is bass, bass and more bass.

Kate and I heard about Ronnie and Dave from Glenda Mink who showed us around Polk County and introduced us to the entertainment that was on offer; with temperatures in the high eighties or low nineties the fun was outside on the water, fishing, skiing, swimming or boating. One night Kate and I were sitting outside by the swimming pool having a midnight drink before turning in when the phone rang:

'Are you Martin James from England?'

'That's me,' I answered.

'I'm Ronnie Waggers. You wanna go fishing in the morning for bass?'

I said we did, and arranged that Kate and I would meet him at 5 a.m. This gave us just four hours sleep before we had to shower and put on our shorts, T-shirts and trainers, and meet our guide. Talk about a cheerful guy: Ronnie was full of life . . . and jokes.

Into his four-wheel drive Ford and we were away, first stop the gas station for packs of ice, fresh sandwiches, doughnuts and cans of cold drink. 'Wanna coffee and fresh doughnut?' asked Ronnie. We both did, and so we all sat there at dawn in the quiet of the Florida countryside having an early snack. What a life! We could suffer this for the next few months!

Ronnie told us we were off to the phosphate pits complex, a series of lakes that he and Dave manage as a wildlife and angling centre on behalf of a large mining company. I was impressed with the way companies and individuals cared for the environment; as a people, we could learn a lot. In Florida you don't have to worry about dog dirt and litter, the menace of the nineties in England, because Floridians get together to keep their streets and countryside clean; they even adopt roads, either as a group or as individuals. They all care – the churches, scouts, anglers, schools, girl guides, environmentalists, hunters – and they get involved; it's their future and their children's future they are protecting. Anglers will adopt a boat dock and ensure that it is kept clean, because there are always idiots who dump their rubbish at the end of a fishing trip; that happens the world over. But it is only the minority in the United States, whereas it seems it is the majority in the UK; that is the difference.

After a drive of half an hour we arrived at the Pits, as they are known. Ospreys and eagles were wheeling on the thermals; egrets were everywhere. At the water's edge we found two large eyes peering just above the surface; they belonged to one of the many alligators that inhabit these pits. They are sometimes transferred from lake to lake for restocking, just as we restock with fish.

In no time at all the boat was in the water, all 20,000 dollars' worth packed with everything an angler might need. Ronnie's professionally built boat was designed with the bass angler in mind. It was equipped with an aerated live bait tank with controlled water temperature, an ice-box for food and drink, an electric outboard controlled by the foot forward and reverse so that it could turn on a sixpence, an echo sounder, a temperature gauge, a fish finder, a fire extinguisher, padded swivel seats, extra batteries and storage for rods and so on, and wet weather gear should you need it. It was a work of art and, to top all that, it was equipped with a 50 hp outboard motor with an electric starter.

We climbed in; what lovely padded seats! On with our life vests, and then Ronnie started the motor. We moved off slowly; then the throttle was opened, the bows lifted from the water and we skimmed away to a distant mark. The temperature was already in the eighties, the sky was blue and the water calm. We were off bass fishing, American-style, and we loved it.

As we neared the first mark, the big engine was shut down and Ronnie switched over to the electric trolling motor. All was peace and quiet. The other electronics were switched on and we moved slowly around looking for drop-offs and underwater snags where the fish might be lying up. We found a place where trees were growing in the water, and decided it was time to fish. Ronnie handed Kate a spinning outfit baited with a plastic worm; he and I fished with short bait-casting rods and multiplier reels using floating plugs. We cast around the trees where we hoped the fish would be lying in ambush.

Ronnie's rod buckled over: he was into the first fish of the day. Soon a nice bass was being lifted from the water, a fish of about four pounds, and this only ten minutes after starting. Kate then had a good fish grab her plastic worm just under the surface; the rod stabbed down to the water and line was pulled from the reel.

'Get the rod up, Kate! That's a good fish,' I shouted. Then Ronnie took over giving Kate instruction, and soon a super 5lb bass was lifted into the boat. It was Kate's first, and she was all smiles. In the next couple of hours, with just the alligators, eagles and ospreys for company, we tried several spots and caught plenty of fish. The temperature was now 88°F: time for more sun-cream and a cold drink. Then another bass hit my top water lure, and tail-walked with its gills flaring. This was real fun fishing, and as an added bonus we had the sunshine. Soon we were each into a good fish, all three rods buckling over as we fought America's number one fish in gin-clear water under an azure sky.

I've done a lot of bass fishing since those first days, and I must say it is always great fun.

Florida has another great attraction: its coastline, and two areas in particular spring to mind: the Keys and the Gulf of Mexico. Maybe I wasn't destined to fish the Keys for bonefish and tarpon, because weather problems in the form of a hurricane arrived a couple of days before my planned visit. Dick Pope, who is a former holder of the world bonefish record and a very experienced all-round angler in fresh- and saltwater, had offered to act as my guide for a trip to the Keys, but the weather beat me. Maybe my time will come.

THE GULF OF MEXICO

I was sitting at a bar in Hooters' Restaurant in Lakeland one day minding my own business when a slim, suntanned man came across and introduced himself.

'Hi, I'm Jim Decker. I listened to your talk yesterday and found it most interesting.'

We shook hands and I asked him to sit down. The conversation turned to fishing, and Jim asked if Kate and I fancied a trip out into the Gulf for a bit of fishing with his wife Ammy and himself. He would also invite Ron Clifford of Skiaway. (Ron taught me to water-ski.)

Ron Clifford collected Kate and me at about 5 a.m., and we headed west towards Tampa and our eventual destination of Clearwater. The weather was fine, but as we got closer to the coast the wind picked up. Traffic was light, with most motorists observing the speed limit, and we made good time. On the way, Ron told us that he was the world barefoot ski champion and a top aerobatics performer on water-skis; he often performed at Sea World and Cypress Gardens.

In no time we were at the docks. Talk about a millionaires' playground! This place had everything for the water sportsman. What was impressive was the size of each craft and how many there were. Berthed in its own dock, Jim's 45-foot boat was like a floating hotel; it had sleeping cabins with showers, a day cabin with fridge and freezer, a galley and an engine room with twin diesel motors. There was a fighting chair with footrest fitted in the stern. Up on the flying bridge, the electronics included state-of-the-art two-way radio, radar, fish finders and depth sounders. There was even an on-board computer that could monitor the course, speed and fuel consumption.

The comfort of the angler was well provided for, with television, padded swivelling seats, full life-saving equipment, life-raft, wet-weather gear, in fact everything you could ask for. The boat can stay at sea for long periods, which was something Jim and his friends often did, even refuelling at sea. Captain Smith was the man who looked after the boat; he had worked for Jim's father, and he was a very experienced skipper and a great companion to be with.

We had one problem . . . you've guessed it: the weather. The forecast was for gale-force winds, the story of my life when it comes to getting afloat off the Florida coastline. It was suggested we go out into the bay and fish with light tackle for Spanish mackerel, which sounded like good fun, so the engines were switched on and mooring ropes freed. The captain was up on the flying bridge as we left the dock, passing lots of pelicans on the way. As we motored seawards I noticed float planes among the other craft, indicating that their owners must fly down for the weekend.

Out in the gulf we hit rough weather. Dolphins played around, and a pair of them followed us out. Jim's wife Ammy made us tea and toast; I was ready for breakfast. We sat in the cabin talking about baseball, the state of the world and, in particular, how the top American football match would go later in the day. One of the teams was Florida College, so there was lots of local interest. Meanwhile Ammy and Kate decided to go up top to the flying bridge, and within half an hour we had turned for port: it seemed that the girls would rather go shopping than get thrown around all day!

I didn't blame them for their choice: it was rough, and certainly not ideal weather for a boat trip. We dropped them off and returned to sea. As we sailed out into the Gulf it seemed as if the wind was dropping a little, and we trolled for Spanish mackerel until we had caught our limit of ten each. The American saltwater sportsman is also conservation-minded.

Captain Smith shouted down from the bridge, 'Barracuda forty yards astern! It's a big fish.' We all jumped into action, bringing in our lightweight rods and storing them safely in their racks. Jim shouted, 'This one's for you, Martin!'

At last I was hopeful of tangling with this fearsome tiger of the sea, with its powerful chopping jaws. Barracuda are a fine fighting fish, often leaping clear of the water and streaking off in fast runs. Sometimes called the sea pike, they are the street fighters of the sea, mean machines which care not a jot for the angler or his tackle and which will hit most baits. This one jumped again thirty yards astern. A fresh Spanish mackerel was fixed on the hooks, while Ron trailed a big popper to keep the 'cuda interested. Was this to be my lucky day? I paid out the bait to the required spot as instructions were fed to me via the skipper and Jim. The motor was on trolling speed.

'Here he comes!' shouted the skipper. The adrenalin was coursing through my body, then I spotted the fish, and it was big. Very big!

'Over four feet,' from the bridge. I desperately wanted this 'cuda that I had waited so long for. He rolled a few yards astern of the bait and I willed him to take it. My heart beat faster, sweat rolled off my brow, my mouth was dry and burning, my eyes were stinging and the sun burnt down fiercely. This was fishing at its best and I braced myself.

'Strike!' the skipper shouted, and I heaved back the rod . . . nothing! Dropping the rod tip down towards the fish, I took in the slack line and struck again. Still nothing! I was gutted. What had gone wrong?

The skipper shouted down, 'The 'cuda's hit the bait.' I was shaking. My chance had gone, and I wound in. The bait had been cut clean in two, half an inch from the hooks, and the cut was as clean as if it had been made by a butcher's knife. How unlucky can you get?

I hope it won't be too long before my dream of catching a 'cuda comes true, perhaps with a big fish off Australia or Dubai. We shall have to see.

CANADA, THE LAST WILDERNESS

Canada is a huge chunk of land and water that stretches from Nova Scotia on the Atlantic coast to British Columbia on the Pacific coast. To the south are the prairie provinces of Manitoba, Saskatchewan and Alberta; travelling north you come to the Precambrian shield and then the North-West Territories, the Tundra and the Arctic Circle. It is a land of awesome beauty with great forests, huge lakes, and superb rivers and streams. It is probably the last great wildlife and angling refuge in the world. Flying across Canada from east to west or north to south I sit and wonder if what I see is land in water, or water in land: there must be hundreds of thousands of lakes, and all holding fish. Furthermore, the fishing is really an unknown quantity, as many waters have only been fished by the local Indians and the Inuits – in fact many have probably never been fished at all.

As a writer and broadcaster, and as travel consultant to Maggi Smit's company Go Fishing Canada, I have had the opportunity to fish in all of Canada's provinces, and with great success. If your interest is in catching Atlantic salmon then you could do no better than to visit the Miramichi; this river is world famous for its salmon fishing, and flows through the heartland of New Brunswick. It is quite beautiful, clear water running over a succession of gravel bars and into channels, flowing through oxbows with fertile islands, and backwaters known locally as 'bogans', providing habitat for beaver and otter. One October dawn I was at Ponds' Resort. Mist was rising from the water, there was a heavy frost underfoot, and as I looked up the pool I could see five anglers each playing a salmon: such is the calibre of fishing available on the Miramichi, and it is improving all the time because anglers practise catch and release, and nets have been taken off the estuary. This should be a lesson to all of us, to do as the Canadians do.

Kate caught her first salmon in Canada, but not from the Miramichi. We were in Nova Scotia on the Margaree, and the water level was ideal. However, although four of us fished hard on the first day we had no success, though we could see plenty of fish in the pools. Then on the second day we had been fishing for about three hours when Kate shouted that she was into a fish which had taken her fly, a green-butt skunk. I grabbed my camera and tape recorder, determined not to let this moment escape without record, and soon Kate had a lovely clean salmon on the bank: her first, and the only one we caught (although a local angler did take fish of 24lb and 18lb that very day). In fact the Margaree produces a lot of fish each year, yet the fishing is available for just the price of a rod licence.

One year we visited Manitoba, with its countless unspoiled lakes and rivers. This time our destination was North Knife Lake Lodge in the north of the province, in a very beautiful setting and reached by float plane from Thompson. The lake is some thirty miles long by eight miles wide and is dotted with islands, and it offers excellent fishing for lake trout, Arctic grayling and pike. The lake trout grow to almost 5lb, and many of the pike exceed 20lb and give tremendous sport. For best results you need to use either bait-casting tackle and floating plugs or fly-fishing tackle and big flies (sizes 4/0 and 5/0).

The lake had risen a foot, and the lake trout and pike had moved to a river mouth one morning when Kate and I, with Glen our guide, left the boat dock to seek them out. Half an hour later we were ready to fish, Kate and Glen with spinning tackle and 'five of diamonds' lures, me with a Sage travel rod, size 9 floating line and a size 4/0 polar fly. We moved up into the mouth of the river and fished until we had drifted out of range of the trout; then it was back to the river mouth to repeat the process. The fishing was excellent: trout after trout hit our flies and lures and we were really having a ball. There were several instances when we all had fish on at the same time, and these lake trout really could fight. To see a big old lake trout come up and hit a fly as it is twitched slowly across the surface is quite something; and as you play the fish you may have eagles, bears and beavers as company, and you always have the loons. I began to feel it was *too* easy – but then, some anglers are never satisfied: if it's easy we want it hard, and if it's too hard then we complain.

On one occasion after lunch I had a cracking pike of about 20lb take a big fly tied on a size 5/0 hook to represent a mouse. Glen had advised me to cast the fly into a dense weedbed and to let it lie there. After about five minutes there was a boil on the surface and three foot of pike shot skywards, crashed back and then leapt skywards once more, this time tail-walking across the weedbed. Then it dived through the weedbed and into the open water, and the reel screamed fiendishly as the line was ripped down to the last few yards of backing. However, the fish then turned towards me, giving a much-needed chance to get some line back onto the reel. Three or four times the pike changed direction: it was certainly thrilling. Slowly I gained control of the battle, and then Glen had the fish in the net. A quick picture and it was back into the water. What a lovely fish, and what a scrap!

Kate and I have had many good days in Manitoba, and none more so than when we went to the uniquely fascinating town of Churchill. From there we were able to take a trip on a tundra buggy and watch the polar bears out on the tundra. We also saw the beluga whales in the Churchill river: all part of the scene in wildest Canada.

Saskatchewan is the next province going west from Manitoba, the home of Cree Indians, trappers, white-water rafting, grizzly bears, caribou, beaver, bald eagles, and so much more. This province has hundreds of miles of river and over 100,000 lakes; Woolaston lake alone covers more than 800 square miles of water. I love the whole province and have been lucky to spend a lot of time there.

Saskatoon! What a lovely city, with its fine university, the white pelicans on the river, and Wanuskewin Heritage Park. Here you can see how the Indians live, and meet wonderful characters like Wes Fine Day, a Cree Indian chief who kept me interested all day long with his stories.

Minor Bay, on Woolaston lake, is the home of Gerald and Paulette Howard. It is about half an hour's drive from the small airport of Points North, and offers excellent fishing and wildlife spotting. You live in simple log cabins, though all the meals are served in the main cookhouse and the food is excellent – and when you are fishing it's not just cheese sandwiches but a proper shore lunch cooked by your guide. You never go hungry in the Canadian wilderness unless you fail to catch a fish, and to the best of my knowledge that hasn't happened yet.

It was on an ordinary August day that I had a record-breaking catch. I had come to northern Saskatchewan, some 600 miles north of Saskatoon, to fish for pike with a fly rod and a floating line, to prove that the big ones could be taken on a fly at this time of the year. The sun climbed slowly over the pine trees on the opposite shore of Woolaston, a lake so huge that is more like an inland sea. And the fish were huge, too.

As we made our way to the main lodge for breakfast we were greeted by the smell of sizzling bacon and sausages; I was looking forward to some pancakes, too, and maple syrup with my crispy bacon. A mist was rolling off the water; two bald eagles were working for their breakfast; a beaver was making its way home after its nocturnal wanderings; whisky jays were looking for an easy feed – these are as plentiful as starlings in Britain, and they will even come down and take food from your hand. This deep lake was carved by glaciers long ago, and some of the oldest rock in the world surrounds its shores. The clear, cold water provides some of the best fishing in North America. Forty-year-old pike swim beneath these waters and compete to seize any big flies that invade their territory; these fish put up a ferocious fight, head-shaking, tail-walking and going off in fast runs of twenty, thirty yards and more. The reel screams like a demented demon, the rod tip often plunges beneath the surface, and for twenty minutes your heart is in your mouth: they are hard-fighting fish these pike.

Lake trout also abound in the cold waters of Woolaston, and they can be caught throughout the summer; but many of the trophy fish are caught in the spring and fall. These fish also put up a good fight, but not like the pike. In the surrounding lakes Arctic grayling, the sailfish of the north, present the ultimate challenge; you fish for them with light fly-fishing tackle, and when hooked they perform dramatic turns and aerobatic leaps that guarantee you some exciting fishing. All the fishing is done from boats, sturdy 18-foot aluminium craft equipped with 30 hp Evinrude motors, padded seats with back rests and a built-in wooden floor. A large area in the bows of the boat is carpeted to ensure easy shooting of the line.

We reached the boat dock just before eight in the morning. The sun had burnt off the early morning mist and a few whitefish were swirling around in the bay; the water was as smooth as glass and it was great to be alive. However, little did I know what was in store for us during the next few hours. Corrie Howard, our guide, led the way to the boat where we stowed the gear, put on life jackets and settled into the padded seats. One pull of the starter cord and we were away, skimming the glass-like surface, passing small groups of loons and a lone Cree Indian who, like us, was fishing; though he wasn't fishing for sport, but to feed his family. Sometimes we had a Cree Indian guide, and they were certainly knowledgeable about fishing and wildlife, and very entertaining. We would return most of our fish, only keeping one for our shore lunch.

After half an hour, Corrie throttled back the motor as we made a right turn into a four-acre bay, just one tiny area of Woolaston lake; at its edge the water plunged away to a depth of sixty feet, and in the bay itself there were large weedbeds, where hopefully the pike would be at home. Corrie paddled the boat into position so that we could drift down the bay, which allowed me to cast in front of the boat for any patrolling pike. Our tackle had been chosen with great care because we were expecting to catch fish of twenty pounds or more: Sage travel rods designed to handle sizes 9 and 10 lines; big flies dressed on size 4/0 hooks; and an Airflo floating leader to which we attached six feet of 12lb nylon line and twelve inches of 20lb wire – the pike has a mouth full of teeth that are as sharp as razor blades. The polar flies we used were tied up for us by Stu Thompson who runs the fly-tying department at The Fishin' Hole in Winnipeg, a shop as big as a Woolworth's store and stocking everything the angler could ask for, even down to electric hook sharpeners. We had a selection of other large flies, but the polar fly was my first choice as it looks so lifelike in the water; with it we could imitate the bait fish perfectly.

I cast a long line to a gap in the weedbed and retrieved about six feet of line. There was a huge swirl, the rod tip was slammed down to the water, line shot through my fingers and the fight was on: my first fish of the day was taking line off the reel at a terrific rate as it fought for freedom. The combination of well balanced tackle, and finger control on the reel tipped the fight in my favour, and soon I was able to gain some line: inch by inch, and then foot by foot backing was retrieved, and then the fly line, and thus at this point the fight seemed to be going my way – but the pike wasn't finished yet; it had other ideas. It bounded for the bottom and the reel screamed. I eased off the pressure and let the fish burn up energy, and for a moment all was quiet; then once again I was taking in line, and this time the fish was beaten.

Corrie said, 'Well done! It's a good one,' and I had my first look at the fish. It was about 15lb, and what a fighter, far better than our Atlantic salmon of the previous year. If our boxers fought as hard as these pike then we would hold all the world records.

The pike was gently unhooked, and released to grow into a thirty-pounder. I cast the polar fly once more and as it hit the water, there was a swirl. I lifted the rod tip and set the hook into my second fish of the day. This one was different: it reared up out of the water like a Polaris missile and crashed back in a shower of spray; the sun glinting on the water droplets made them look like diamonds. The fight was under way, the fish back on the surface, head-shaking and tail-walking, then making fast spectacular runs. With the sun beating down we could be excused for thinking that we were on the Florida flats fishing for bonefish. But this was no bonefish, it was my second pike in two casts.

Pound for pound these are some of the hardest-fighting fish I have caught in fresh- or saltwater. I wanted more of this action, and during the ten-hour session I had it: Seventy casts and seventy pike, and according to Corrie their total weight was somewhere between 350 and 400lb. I was too busy casting, playing and unhooking fish to keep count. It was my best-ever day's fishing in fifty-one years of angling, and the day was made complete when Kate set her fly into a trophy fish of around 25lb. Several times her rod top was pulled under the water, but she hung on grimly, and after a hard, slogging battle with a mean heavyweight pike, she was able to relax and smile as Corrie held aloft her prize.

That day we shattered the myth upheld by the American angler, which proposes that the fishing is no good in August. 'What is it like in the best months?' I wondered.

OREGON: CLEAN AND GREEN AND LOVELY

On the west coat of the USA between the states of Washington and California is the state of Oregon: it has thousands of miles of rivers and streams, and hundreds of lakes and reservoirs offering most types of freshwater fishing; there are Chinook salmon to over 80lb, stripers to 60lb, and sturgeon well over 500lb with always the possibility of catching one of 1,000lb. Oregon has carp, bass, catfish and many species of trout, and all the salmon species except for the Atlantic salmon. The lower reaches of the Umpqua river provide what is arguably the best smallmouth bass river fishing in the United States; it was also on this river that in May 1993 I caught shad of 5lb on a small rubber jig (the shad is a hard-fighting fish, the poor man's tarpon). From the border of Washington state in the north, to California in the south, are hundreds of miles of beaches that provide excellent fishing. In fact Oregon offers everything a fisherman could possibly want, and there is plenty for the rest of the family.

The number one fish in the United Kingdom is the carp; and in Oregon, too, it is present in large numbers. The fishing is free, and the carp grow to perhaps 50lb, and yet it is a species that many Oregon anglers regard as vermin; on the Snake river, that flows along the border between Oregon and Idaho, I've seen carp of 40lb swimming around as if they hadn't a care in the world.

Jackie Smith of Originally Oregon, a travel company based in Kent, arranged my trip. I hadn't gone just for the fishing: it was the 150th anniversary of the Oregon trail, and I was to do a series of radio programmes. It was also an ambition of mine to fish the Rogue, Deschutes and Umpqua rivers that had been fished by such famous people as Zane Grey, Roderick Haig-Brown and Jim Schollmeyer. I arrived at Gatwick Airport for my Northwest Airlines flight, and while I was there, recorded a piece about the Boeing 747-400. Flying today is so much more enjoyable than it was twenty years ago: the food is good, the seats comfortable and there is even on-board entertainment if you don't want to read or admire the views.

First stop was St Paul, Minnesota, where over coffee I recorded an interview

David Stirling, who founded the Long-Range Desert Group during the Second World War – later to become the SAS – with ex-President Ronald Reagan.

With Bernard Venables, admiring Bernard's famous Crabtree net.

It took me nearly forty years to catch a two-pound Kennet roach like this one.

The Richard Walker trophy was awarded to me by the National Association of Specialist Anglers.

My best tench weighed in at just over 8lb; it came from a lake in Gloucestershire.

Kate playing a good fish on North Knife Lake in northern Manitoba.

Chris Yates and me with an eel taken from a Somerset water while carp fishing.

I caught this rudd from a gravel pit at South Cerney. It fell to legered bread crust and weighed over 3lb.

Kate nets another chub for me on the River Ribble where we spend many happy hours fishing in winter. (Picture courtesy of Eaglemoss Publications.)

Mum and Dad with their first
grandchild, Andrew, son of Martin's
brother Ron.

Sharon, my daughter, an air hostess,
who travels further afield than I do.

Another lake trout for Kate.

Tony Farquharson with a pike just
like the one I caught at Teston all
those years ago.

Martin in the cowboy country of Oregon fishing for steelhead at dawn on the Deschutes River. (Photo: Jim Schollmeyer.)

Some members of the Ribble Valley Crossroads Carers at a coffee morning in the mayor's parlour, organized by the author to raise funds; (left to right) Beryl Cassidy, Kathleen Eastwood, Martin James, President Lady Clitheroe and Roy Dewhurst.

A brace of cod for the author, fishing in shallow water with 12lb line and a carp rod.

with Doug Killian of Northwest Airlines. He told me that the walleye is one of the most popular fish in the northern states. Then it was time to board another flight for Seattle in Washington state, and a chance to get a good view of Mount St Helen, the volcanic mountain that erupted in 1982 and caused weather problems worldwide. From the airport, a four-hour drive brought us to the Heathman Hotel in Portland. I arrived at midnight, and it seemed that no sooner had my head hit the pillow than the telephone rang and a sweet young voice said, 'Your alarm call, Mr James. Its 6.30 a.m.' – I was having one of those lovely dreams about catching a big steelhead. Or was it a sturgeon?

I staggered out of bed and into the shower. It's surprising what a shower does for the system: soon I was dressed and ready for the day. After breakfast I set off for the Columbia river to fish for sturgeon – at least that's what I'd hoped, but when I got there I learnt that you aren't allowed to fish for sturgeon unless you have bought a special tag, which must be attached to your licence.

All was not lost, as my licence did allow me to fish for non-migratory rainbow trout. So after a telephone call, it was off to the Deschutes river in central Oregon, a three-hour drive through lovely countryside on highway 26 to Warm Springs Indian reservation. There I met my guide Rick Killingworth of the High Desert Drifters. Rick organizes what are called 'float trips' on his Mackenzie river boat. As you drift down this lovely river canyon you pass beneath massive sandstone cliffs which tower above the river. At any moment you might expect to see John Wayne, or Roy Rogers and Trigger: it is that type of countryside. I saw red-tailed hawks, bald eagles, golden eagles, turkey vultures, red-winged blackbirds, yellow-headed blackbirds, meadowlarks, mergansers, ospreys, chukars, bobcats, otters, mink, muskrats and porcupine.

The redsides are rainbow trout, and on the Deschutes river they range from twelve to twenty inches, with the occasional larger fish. On most of the river the fishing is open all year round. The regulations prohibit fishing from a boat, and so good wading gear is essential for a safe and fun-filled trip – but forget thigh waders, they are useless: chest waders are a must. I wear stocking-foot neoprene chest waders with a good pair of wading boots with felt soles and cleats. And if you visit the Deschutes during the summer months, take a pair of shorts to wear under your waders; this is a high desert country, and the temperatures can get to 100°Fahrenheit. The Deschutes is a catch-and-release river, and if you are fishing for steelhead then you need steelhead tags. Licences and tags for different species of fish are available from most tackle stores.

Our plan was to drift and fish our way downriver to Trout Creek, a trip of some ten miles. Rick sorted out the boat while I put on my chest waders and wading boots. I set up my 9 foot 6 inch Sage travel rod with a size 7 floating line, 9-foot leader tapering to a 6lb point, and a girdle bug nymph with rubber legs. The water was a foot above normal, and it needed a BB shot twelve inches from the nymph to get down to the bottom.

All was now ready, and we started our first drift, going through a class one (gentle) rapid and on for two miles until we stopped at an island. It was time to go fishing. I stepped over the side of the boat into waist-deep swirling water, and moved cautiously away from the boat so that I would be in a good position for fishing upstream. Then, pulling some line off the reel, I began casting and retrieving as best I could. However, it was soon obvious that I was making a real pig's ear of the job. My casts were awkward, my wading clumsy, and for the first half hour I struggled; then Rick gave me some help and I began to get my act together, though it still felt strange to cast a fly with split shot on the line. But another half hour and I was into the rhythm: casting, retrieving, taking a step upstream, casting, retrieving, and then another step upstream.

Cast, retrieve and move – that was the tactic, and it worked. I had a few pulls, but they were like greased lightning. Then I spotted the bite indicator move, and I struck. A fish was on, scrapping like a demon in the fast water. Soon I was able to reach down and unhook my first Deschutes river fish, sadly not a redside but a whitefish, rather like our grayling though without the big dorsal fin. After a few more casts I went back to the boat and we moved downstream under highway 26 bridge, through another rapid. There Rick said, 'This is a fine area for redsides,' and pulled the boat into the bank.

Once more it was into the icy, fast-running water, but now I knew what to expect and I was ready when the current hit me. I waded out from the boat, pulled off a few yards of line and cast a line upstream. On the fifth cast I had a pull and missed. I cast again, and once more missed my chance. The bite indicator moved, I made a rapid strike and a fish was taking line through my fingers. I had to let it go, such was the power of the fish as it shot off downstream; the rod hooped over, the reel screamed and the line shot through the rings. Then the knot joining the backing appeared; this too was going away fast.

I began to stumble and wade downstream, trying to follow the fish. A trout jumped some thirty yards downstream. 'That's your fish, Martin!' Rick shouted. 'It's a good redside.'

That only made matters worse, and I started to worry about losing this fish I had travelled thousands of miles for. But then the trout kited into the bank and I began gaining line; and after a wonderful scrap the fish was mine. Rick didn't use a landing net: he bent down and cradled the fish in his hands and the hook fell out easily. We took a picture and released the redside with its head facing upstream. The trout rested a while and then, having pumped oxygen back into its body, moved off strongly.

It was time for a bite to eat, and we scrambled onto the river bank – and that was when I heard the sound everyone dreads when in desert country, the buzz, buzz of a prairie rattlesnake, and it was just a foot or so in front of me, ready to strike. This one was brown with light markings and about three feet long. I grabbed the tape recorder and taped the sound of its rattle; then I dropped the microphone onto its tail, and when I played the tape back in the studio I could hear Rick saying, 'Be careful, Martin, it's ready to strike!'

Two other snakes that you can expect to see in Oregon are the gopher and the garter; both are harmless, but they can give you a fright if you don't see them until you are right upon them. However, one bush you don't touch if you can help it is the poison oak, because it gives off an oily substance that brings you out in a very painful rash which lasts for up to a fortnight. There is no cure except time, although the doctor can make it less painful. Dave Hughes in his book *Deschutes* writes, 'My policy now when on the Deschutes is to use pumice soap every evening, even if I've just seen poison oak going by in the distance. I don't trust it.'

In October of that year I returned once more to Oregon to appear on TV and to take part in radio interviews and an hour-long phone-in programme. I was also going to do some fishing, and I hoped to catch a steelhead trout. The first few days were spent working in the Portland area, recording interviews for my tea-time show, but I also visited Danner Boots who make some of the best wading boots available; Kauffmann's Streamborn, one of the top fly-fishing shops in the States; and Caddis who make float tubes. Having done some float tubing in May, I had become interested in this form of fishing, and could foresee plenty of opportunity to use a float tube in the UK and Ireland.

Then it was off to the Big K Ranch to fish the lower Umpqua river for smallmouth bass; I also hoped to catch a Chinook salmon and a steelhead. The Big K is an ideal location for the family holiday: there is plenty of open space; you sleep in timber cabins and eat in a main dining-room; the food is good and plentiful; and, most important for fishermen, there are ten miles of river to fish. I fished with fly and spinner, catching plenty of smallmouth bass, a small steelhead and a jack salmon. The steelhead was only fifteen inches long, so it didn't really count. I was able to watch otters and beavers at play – one morning I watched an otter catch a 5lb salmon – and there were elk, deer, wild turkeys, eagles, ospreys and lots of waterfowl.

My next stop was the north Umpqua, where I spent a few days with Frank and Jeanne Moore who built the Steamboat Inn. This area of the Umpqua was made famous in the 1920s by Zane Grey and Major Mott. The river flows through a gorge with huge Douglas firs, cedars and hemlocks, some of these being over 600 years old and 250 feet high. It is eagle and osprey territory, and what more could an angler ask for – except perhaps a fish. I fished the river from dawn to dusk, and in three days I had just two trout rise to the fly; only one took the fly, and I missed it. But it was magnificent just being there and fishing.

STEELHEAD OF THE DESCHUTES

My journey took me next to the city of Bend where I recorded a TV programme, *An Englishman's View of Oregon*. I then went on to Redsides Lodge on the Deschutes river and met my host for the next couple of days, Herman Jordan. Herman had spent most of his life on a working cattle ranch, running cattle, branding, growing food, making hay and doing the thousand and one jobs a cowboy is called upon to do: it's not at all like the films. Along with the rest of the family Herman had been taught how to cook, and the food we had was excellent. My guide was photographer, writer, naturalist and angler, Jim Schollmeyer, and I couldn't have had a better teacher.

After breakfast it was into chest waders and boots and away to Warm Springs Indian reservation where we were soon out on the river, stopping here and there to fish; and what fun we had catching whitefish and redsides. In the afternoon I was back on the river casting for a steelhead, but without even a pull from a fish. We got back into the boat and drifted further down the stream, stopping at an area of fast shallow water. I was soon out of the boat and fishing, and at last I felt a take. I struck, and a good redside fought like a wild thing. I was able to unhook it in the water. Having checked my tackle for wind knots, I cast upstream once more and worked my team of flies back towards me. I noticed the line move a fraction, and I tightened. As I did so I felt the powerful surge of a big fish. It jumped twice. Another redside, I thought, and a big one. Then it jumped again, and I could see it was a fish of between 6 and 8lb.

'Steelhead, Martin!' Jim shouted. The fish shot off downstream, jumped again and crashed back in a shower of spray; I began to tremble as I realised that at last I had got to grips with a steelhead. But this fish was running on rocket fuel. As it again leapt skywards once more it shone in the sunlight like a bar of silver, and then crashed back sending rippling circles out across the river.

The fly line shot through the rod rings in a blur, and was followed by the green backing; I struggled to prevent the rod tip thumping down into the water as the fish twisted and plunged at the end of the line. But then the rod thumped over from butt to tip as if a giant had grabbed hold of it, and I could even feel the bend in the cork handle; the rod tip was pulled down to the water, and I had to let the fish take it back again, and every now and then I had to cling to Jim so that I could rest my aching arms. My hands were going numb, but no way was I going to give in to this fish. Then, as I regained more of the backing the fly line appeared: I was winning my fight with a fish that had recently come in from the sea and which seemed desperate to get back there. Then all went slack: the fish was off. The size 16 nymph was missing.

I felt gutted, as if my house had burned down or my book collection had been stolen. I felt empty, my stomach was all knotted and I was all of a tremble. I had not felt like this for many years.

By now the sun had slipped below the canyon rim, and I felt a chill breeze on my neck. One or two stars had appeared, and then a bat came out looking for an early supper. The sky above me was ice blue: there would be a heavy frost by dawn. The new moon appeared, and then a big fish rolled on the surface. Under the far bank two otters appeared, and I heard a distant scream, probably a small rodent caught by an owl. It was time to get back in the boat for the last drift down to Trout Creek.

Oregon and Jim Schollmeyer had certainly given me an exciting day, and one I would not forget in a hurry.

CHAPTER 6

Both Barrels

October

The hazy sunshine filters down
To greet an autumn day,
A crisp and bright October morn;
Gentle breezes play.
The crunch of leaves beneath your feet,
Shades of gold and brown,
The fading colours of Nature's coat,
Swept across the ground.
Amber, yellow, a glow of red,
Strewn at random lay,
All make up the golden scene,
When St Luke has his day.
Above the rustle of the trees,
As each branch sheds its last,
The air feels cold upon your face,
The season soon to pass.

Lorraine Davies

Ever since getting my first Webley air-rifle in 1946 I have been interested in shooting as a sport, and I have enjoyed being out with dog and gun in the fields and marshes of the British Isles. If it wasn't for the big shooting estates a lot of our countryside might well be covered in asphalt, housing estates and factories. However, my shooting ended in 1987 when I found myself back in a wheelchair owing to my multiple sclerosis. No longer could I exercise my yellow labrador, Nell, and so I had no choice but to ask my friend John Halstead to find a good home for her. John was a field trials champion and a top-class trainer of gun-dogs, and he was able to place Nell with a retired doctor who went picking up and shooting three or four days a week; so Nell was able to carry on doing what she did best. I decided that even if my condition improved my shooting days were over. I no longer shoot, but I do cherish some lovely memories from the past forty-odd years.

Winter has meant so many delights: duck shooting at dawn, driven pheasant shooting in the afternoon, decoying pigeons over the green crops in the snow, rabbiting with dog and gun or ferrets and nets. I've experienced what to me are the most exciting sounds of all: the call of the wild goose on the Solway marshes, on the Wash estuary, on the hills and fields of Perthshire, and on the wetlands of Ireland; and the purr and whistle of the widgeon under the moon on the Ouse washes and the Medway marshes.

SOME RABBITING MEMORIES

During the late 1940s and through the 1950s I spent a lot of my time with air-rifle and shotgun, walking the hedgerows or crawling across meadows in search of rabbits. They are a fine sporting quarry and I rate them as highly as any; only a snob would turn up his nose at a day's rabbiting, something which demands greater skill than does, say, driven pheasant shooting. Many of the guns at driven pheasant shoots are not true country lovers; for them the shoot is more a social occasion, a place to clinch a business deal, rather like a game of golf.

On a summer's evening I would stalk rabbits with all the concentration of a deer stalker in a Scottish glen. Many a time I would turn up for school with ferrets in my pockets and nets in my satchel among the maths and English books, hoping I might bag a couple of rabbits on my way home. I flighted ducks and geese, attended the more formal pheasant shoots, decoyed pigeons, and joined the countywide roosting pigeon shoots in February. All this was in addition to my fishing. Where did I find the time, I often wonder?

Rabbits were certainly my favourite quarry, and they do make excellent eating; I hunted them by day and by night all through the year. I remember going on one camping and fishing trip to the River Beault with a couple of mates. We had little money to spend on food, and we were also some way from the shops, but we didn't worry: we could still live like princes, because the farmer had said we could use our air-rifles to shoot rabbits, and we always had a few snares. We also intended catching a few perch. So on the first night we set our snares and had two rabbits; one we cooked for breakfast and one for supper: delightful! During that two-week trip we had rabbit every day, either fried or stewed with some spuds and anything else we could scrounge, and always with a couple of Oxo cubes thrown in for good measure.

In the sixties my rabbiting days were almost ended because of that dreadful disease myxomatosis. We even heard tales of infected rabbit ears being dumped in areas of the countryside where the disease had not yet reached. What a dreadful thing to do! Almost all the farmers and market gardeners I knew regarded the rabbit as a pest, but they still considered it abhorrent that people were prepared to spread this disease. Thankfully rabbits are now back, and a new generation of youngsters has the chance to stalk a rabbit during the school holidays.

In the late forties there was a lot of pocket money to be made from selling rabbits, because other types of meat were rationed. Our local butcher, for example, would take all we could get, and the neighbours used to call on my friends and me and book their Sunday dinner. Mind you, we had a few encounters with local gamekeepers, and although we were never caught, we had some narrow escapes. But even at ten years of age we knew how to keep one step ahead of the keeper by having our mates act as decoys. Our hunting ground was the hundreds of acres of Cobham woods, and there we would camp for days on end, living off whatever we could get. I had some good deals going for me: one was with the ironmonger in Strood, who would swap cartridges for rabbits; another was with Mr Doughty who had a fishing tackle shop in Rochester and who would give me hooks in exchange for a rabbit. However, it was a long walk with a gun and a dead rabbit to where he lived, so I would usually shoot a rabbit in the orchard close by, wait for things to quieten down, then hide the gun in the hedgerow and with rabbit under my jacket, make a quick dash to Mr Doughty's.

I'm glad I was a schoolboy during the 1940s and early 1950s; these without doubt were the best years. Today's youngsters miss out on the country sports scene. For one, too many of the adults who are out and about in the countryside fishing, shooting and ferreting, don't seem to care about the youngsters, some even tell me they go out to get away from children, maintaining that children at the waterside or in the country are a nuisance. How selfish can you get?

Even as an adult I still loved to go rabbiting. What joyful dawn stalking sessions I had in the summer of 1985, for example: with my .22 air-rifle fitted with a telescopic sight I would go in search of young rabbits. They would be paunched, skinned and jointed, then taken back for breakfast that day and the surplus for freezing; either way they ended up being fried or grilled and served with crispy bacon and French bread, with a big mug of tea to wash it all down. Even today if a friend brings me a rabbit, I will make a rabbit pie with lots of gravy; it's a meal that takes some beating.

ON A MEDWAY MARSH

With the close season for inland ducks and geese beginning on 1 February, the shooting on my beloved Ouse Washes and Fens was over until September; so Paul Johnson and I headed for a tidal saltmarsh. There, below the high water mark, we could shoot ducks. After a tiring row across the creek, we moored up the dinghy and made the long trek, slipping and sliding, across the mudflats, all the while trying to steer clear of the soft spots. It wasn't easy in the darkness with the rain beating into our faces, but eventually we got settled into our hides, ready and waiting for the dawn flight.

Wind shrieked through the netting of the hide, and the rain on my thorn-proof jacket sounded like a rat-tat-tat of a machine gun; it had been a long time since Paul and I were out in a north-westerly force 9, gusting to 10. The estuary looked drab and grey, the tide was well out, and white horses rolled along the Medway; in the distance a container ship headed for the windswept open sea and perhaps warmer climes. The tide had started to flood, and soon we could see large groups of widgeon trying to find shelter in one of the many creeks into which the sea was flooding. In these conditions high water could be up to an hour early, and the height of the tide another three feet or more above what the tide table had predicted. I made a mental picture of my way back to the sea wall, realising that soon the creek would be full and very rough. I also tried to make mental notes of where the mud turned from the usual porridge type to the oily viscosity that signalled danger if you walked into it on a flooding tide. Tidal saltmarshes can be very dangerous and must be treated with great respect.

In the hide we set about fixing 12oz leads to the decoy anchor lines; 4oz leads may be fine on the Ouse Washes, but on a Medway saltmarsh you need much more weight. Then with our waders pulled up high, we began to put out the decoys which was easier said than done because they kept dragging their moorings in the gale-lashed water. Then icy water hit my thighs, and for a moment I was so shocked that I couldn't move as the rising water flooded into my waders. Regaining my senses, I completed the work of setting the 'coys, and returned to the sanctuary of the hide; there I turned down the waders and water gushed out: a second cold blast shot through the nether regions. I settled down, loaded my Blands 3-inch magnum with two shells carrying size 5 shot, and waited.

Out of the gloom, beating through the heavy rain, came the first duck of the flight – not a widgeon as I had expected, but a drake mallard. I put up the gun and, as I did so, heard Paul fire twice. Then I was up and swinging through; I pulled the trigger, heard the thump and saw a mallard crash on the mud ten yards out from the hide. I retrieved this one myself. Meanwhile Paul had scored a right and left with widgeon. My next two shots were at half-a-dozen teal that streaked through the rain to the decoys. Thump, thump, missed! They flared upwards and away.

The next two shots were taken while the tide was flooding the exposed mudflats and half-a-dozen widgeon appeared over the decoys. Up with the gun, and I pulled both triggers. Missed! On to the next bird . . . swing through . . . pull. A hit! A fine cock widgeon was blown by the wind to crash on the other side of the creek. It was time for Druid, my labrador, to earn his keep, and soon the widgeon joined the mallard in the hide.

Four hours into the flood tide, and ducks flew thick and fast. I bagged another four widgeon, two mallard and a teal, but fired forty-eight shells. Then with the wind still as strong, we decided to make our way back – and what a rough crossing of the creek we had! But it had been a bonus day's shooting, and it was great to smell the saltmarsh once again. As Paul said to me on the way home, 'This is real shooting, not like your pampered pheasant shooters'.

I've always maintained that saltmarsh wildfowling with the tide and the mud is what wildfowling is all about. Just to gather round a small flightpond, or to shoot ducks on the river at dusk isn't the real thing at all. Living in Kent, I had some of the best wildfowling in the country, shooting the Thames and Medway estuaries, from both the Kent and the Essex sides.

HUNTING IN THE SNOW

It was mid-January, and I was discussing with policeman Rodney Gooderson of Upwell near Wisbech the abnormally mild conditions, and how neither the North West nor the Fens had yet been ravaged by Arctic weather. But we both agreed we needed to get through the rest of January and February before we could start thinking we had had a mild winter; rough weather could still strike – and it did, just a week later; as the blizzards swept south from Scotland, the Lancashire countryside was covered by snow. I was in Sussex with my old mate John Bodsworth, collecting material for one of my field sports programmes; the weather was bright and sunny when I left John's on 23 January, but by the time I had reached the M11 there was heavy rain and a strong wind. I was heading for the Ouse Washes at Welney for an evening flight at the widgeon, and when I arrived in Cambridgeshire the countryside had a covering of snow.

As I got out of the car, the cold north-easterly hit me square in the face; obviously on this flight I would need my white boilersuit for camouflage. Druid was more creamy-white than yellow, so he would be no problem. Conditions were ideal for duck shooting: wind and falling snow in my experience always keep the ducks flying low, so I was quickly into warm clothes and waders, topped off with my white boilersuit; then with Druid at my side, I made my way across the washes to the hide. It was snowing heavily. I wondered whether the car would get bogged down, but decided to carry on.

Arriving at the stretch of water in front of the hide, I set out the decoys, moved into the hide for cover, and loaded the 12-gauge magnum with 3-inch sixes as I expected to take my birds close in. But what a shocking flight it turned out to be: just three shots at widgeon, and all missed; one I should really forget, but I still enjoyed the experience.

At 6 p.m. and with snow still falling, I started the car for what turned out to be a hair-raising journey north. Several cars had skidded off the road, and I had one bad scare when I slid into the bank, though thankfully the packed snow saved me from injury and the car from damage. Once on the A1 at Newark the weather improved, and Druid and I got to Lancashire around midnight with just one stop for food on the way.

The next day dawned very grey, windy and snowing, just as the weathermen had forecast. With the morning free I decided to try for a few rabbits; for me there has always been something special about hunting rabbits in the snow. I arrived at my small shoot on the banks of the Ribble near Clitheroe after a slow journey through the heavy snow, but with no problems on the road because I was road-testing a four-wheel-drive vehicle. I was using a Winchester 23 side-by-side double barrel, with Three Crowns size 6 shotgun shells which were ideal because I expected the quarry to be at close range; I find that rabbits usually sit tight in snow conditions until flushed by the dog. At the first clump of rushes, a beautiful cock pheasant shot skywards, and I was lucky to drop him with the first shot. But then my luck changed: in the next two hours I had eleven shots at rabbits, and missed them all. Druid was looking at me with disgust.

On arriving at the river I flushed a pair of mallard and scored with a right and left; both ducks crashed into the Ribble, and Druid waited for the order to get on. After a couple of minutes I sent him for the retrieve, and soon these two had joined the pheasant in the gamebag. No bread and jam for me this weekend: I would have some good meals and perhaps make some pâté, too. I returned home well satisfied with my hunting session in the snow.

BACK IN THE FENS

One gunner I used to shoot with was Sam, seventy-two years young, and whom I used to call Old Sam. He was a colourful character, a retired farm worker from Wisbech. Apart from during the war when he was in the army, he had worked on the land since the age of thirteen.

Sam phoned me one Friday night: 'Can you get up tomorrow, boy? The widgeon are in.'

'You bet I can,' I told him, and we agreed to meet by the bridge at Welney. As I headed up the A10 with my Labrador, Jake, wind buffeted the car from side to side. It was perfect weather for shooting ducks, I thought. By 12 noon I was sitting in the Cherry Tree Inn at Welney, enjoying a mug of coffee and a sandwich; it was still blowing hard. Then I heard the sound of Old Sam shouting, 'Have you seen my mate from that there London?'

'Watcha, you old beggar,' I said as we shook hands. Then we were off to

101

the washes where we put on waders and jackets before making our way across the marsh. I put out the decoys and we settled down in the hide. An hour later the birds started to flight in to the decoys, mallard, widgeon and teal. Old Sam was up and swinging his 12-bore across the sky: bang, bang! I looked on in amazement, as those two shots accounted for two beautifully marked teal. 'By Jove,' I thought, 'he moves pretty quick for an old 'un!'

By now, lots of birds were on the wing. My first shot pulled down a cock widgeon, but I missed the next four. Time flew by, and soon it was dark and time for home. Old Sam had shot four teal and eleven widgeon. Me? Just three widgeon.

Old Sam and I fished and shot through the following summer and winter, and the Welney Washes became something of a paradise to me. Then one day during the close season for coarse fishing I received a letter to say that Old Sam had moved to the great hunting lodge in the sky. I sometimes wondered as I dropped a duck on the marshes at Welney if he looked down on me and guided my barrels straight and true.

LOST KEYS

As well as being a keen angler, my friend John Bodsworth also enjoyed shooting; so one January we booked four days together fishing and shooting in Norfolk and on a Monday morning arrived at the Welney Washes. There was plenty of floodwater but we could still reach the hides, and within thirty minutes I was sitting in my wheelchair at our hide while John placed the decoys in a horseshoe shape well within range of our guns. He returned and settled down on an oil-drum, cartridge boxes open, mallard calls and widgeon whistles at the ready.

The dogs sat and waited; my mind went back to Old Sam and I felt a shiver run down my back – I often felt he was standing beside me. I had a similar feeling once on my way back from fishing on the River Ribble, and looking up to the sky said, 'I wish you were at home, mother, so I could come for dinner'. The feeling that night was very strong. I shivered again in the cold dawn air and look skywards. Across the marsh we could hear the whistle and purr of widgeon, and in the distance the quack of a mallard; John answered using the call, and the mallard answered back. The dawn flight had started.

We loaded with sixes in the right barrel and fives in the left. Bang, bang! John had a left and right at teal as they were dropping into the decoys. I missed three shots at widgeon, but was on target with the fourth, bagging one that was going away fast. It fell dead on the other side of the drain, and the dog was sent for it; in no time he was back with it and wearing that look that says, 'There you are, boss'. It was good to see him working.

Duck were flighting everywhere but we missed a lot, due either to poor shooting or to excitement, or perhaps a bit of both. At lunchtime we picked up our empty cartridge cases and threw them into the decoy sack, both feeling thoroughly contented as we tucked into beef sandwiches and coffee. How good the simple things taste when you are out in the open! We relaxed and talked about the morning flight and about other shooting days. The dogs, who had worked so well, were given fresh water to drink and rubbed down.

The afternoon shooting was equally interesting, both of us getting in some cracking shots at tricky birds including a teal which had been ringed in Holland. John also had a teal down beside the hide which we both thought was dead, but half-an-hour later it flew off strongly: it had us fooled, and it served us right for not sending the dog.

By then it was dark, and within an hour, or so we thought, we would be having a hot bath and some dinner. How wrong we were! Having dragged me back to the car, John went back to pick up the decoys only to discover that he had lost the car keys. We phoned the AA who collected the spare keys from John's house, and it was 2.40 a.m. when we got going again.

DUCKS, MUD, WILLOCK AND LEGGET

One of the great things about shooting and fishing is that you meet the nicest of people, and I had the pleasure of shooting with two such like-minded sportsmen back in the late 1950s: Colin Willock and Don Legget. At the time, Colin was angling correspondent of the *Daily Herald* and *The Observer*; Don Legget, a friend of Colin's, was involved in the protective coating of large oil tanks at the Isle of Grain refinery and after his family, it seemed his first love in life was shooting. He was always perfectly dressed, whether in the office or on the marsh. It was arranged that Colin, Don and I would have a few days fowling on the Medway estuary around Upchurch, where the marshes are riddled with creeks and gutters. The mud is like porridge one second and thick black liquid the next and causes all sorts of problems: I have even lost my boots there. Half a mile or so downriver is Dead Man's Island. Oystercatchers and curlews call from overhead, while dunlin, knot and redshank flight to and fro along the tideline. Out on the river you can often see rafts of mallard and widgeon, and on the marsh pools there are usually a few teal ready to rocket skywards when alarmed. It is the perfect place to go wildfowling.

Colin and Don arrived in Rochester one Tuesday lunchtime and booked into the Royal Victoria and Bull Hotel. Don was dressed in a magnificent tweed three-piece shooting suit and wellington boots; it looked as if he had just walked out from a tailor's shop. Colin had driven over in his Morris 1000 Traveller, into which we all piled: three blokes, our dogs and guns – it was that type of motor car – and off we went to the marsh. The Morris 1000 had always been my dream car, but by the time I could afford one the Traveller 1000 was no longer being made, and I couldn't find a secondhand one in good condition. I did own a couple of Morris 1000 saloons, though.

We travelled down the A2 through Gillingham, Rainham and Upchurch; when we arrived at the marsh, the tide was at half flood. There was no wind, it was flat calm and there wasn't a single bird on the wing. Making our way across the marsh, we came to a small creek and squeezed into one of those old-fashioned pram dinghies about ten feet in length. There was just enough room for us all, but it would have been suicidal in rough conditions.

After a short row we landed on the marsh and decided to split up. Don chose a spot where he knew a few ducks would usually flight in most conditions, and settled in with his labrador to await the action. Colin and I went off creek crawling, until the rising tide flooded us off; he moved towards the southern end of the marshy island, while I made the longer trek across the marsh to the seaward side, in the process filling one boot at a deep gutter. However, it was a mild winter's day so I wasn't worried about a boot full of water, a minor thing to put up with when fowling. Across the river I could see the oil refinery. Ocean-going tugs lay at anchor; in the distance a submarine was moored up to a buoy; a few mallard were resting on the water: it wasn't really a wildfowling scene. What we needed was a good north-easterly blowing at least force 8.

Thump, thump! The sound of two shots drifted across from where Legget had settled – it seemed he, at least, was getting some action. I lay there watching the river and hoping that I might also get in a shot or two; the tide was creeping up the marsh, and soon I would have to get back to the other side before the gutters were filled – I didn't fancy a swim. Occasionally a shot could be heard from Colin's shooting area, too: at least my guests were getting some action.

When it was time to return I made my way back to the others, getting in a shot at a teal that jumped from a creek. I found Colin plastered in mud, just as I was; he even had flecks of mud on his glasses. He had shot a brace of teal and a mallard. Don Legget, however, was still spotless, and he had two mallard and two widgeon to boot.

With the water at the top of the marsh, I dragged the dinghy into position, and Don calmly stepped in and sat down. Colin followed. I pushed out the dinghy, got in, took the oars and rowed back to our launching site. We arrived back at the hotel, Don still with the creases in his trousers, Colin and I looking like wildfowlers should, covered in mud and rather damp.

CLIFFE MARSHES

The next day we visited Cliffe marshes for a shoot controlled by one of Colin's friends, a publican who at one time was mine host at the Black Prince in Bexley Heath alongside the A2. I had shot and fished the area for most of my life, and knew it like the back of my hand; in fact as a young teenager I had often crept onto the shoot in the early morning for the dawn flight. Many times I had led the keepers a merry chase, and they hadn't stood a snowball in hell's chance of catching me! Now I was back legally.

The shoot was situated on the inside of the sea wall on the banks of the Thames; on the opposite side was Essex. It was a day of light winds, but the teal shooting was excellent and several times I was able to admire the skilful shooting of Colin and Don – they took only the fast twisting birds. We walked a lot. We shot a hare and some rabbits, and we flushed the occasional pheasant and mallard. Towards dusk we settled into our hides which were fitted with sunken beer barrels – no doubt *borrowed* from the Black Prince – and had a good hour's shooting.

A STICK-IN-THE-MUD

Stoke marshes was an area of really sticky mud, and very dangerous. You had to watch the tide and mud gullies: one problem was the tide filling the creeks and gullies behind you and I have escaped by the skin of my teeth on a couple of occasions. Once when I was nineteen I got trapped in the mud on a flooding tide, and I was really scared: the mud came to above my knees and I couldn't move. Fortunately I was rescued by a local poacher who was walking the sea wall. He helped dig me out, but I lost my BSA single-barrel 12-bore, my boots and all my decoys. It gave me a real fright.

The second incident was when I was cut off by the tide flooding a gully on a freezing January night. I had promised a girl at work a brace of ducks; the tide, however, was being backed up by a strong north-westerly wind and in the darkness I didn't notice the danger, and just sat there hoping to bag a few mallard. Then I noticed white horses rolling up the big creek, and knew I was in trouble; the tide was way above what I had predicted because I had committed the fowler's cardinal sin of ignoring the strength of the wind, which can push up the height of the tide by several feet.

It was going to be a long, hard, cold swim, and I would have to do it without clothes because I knew I couldn't swim this ten-yard creek in these weather conditions with my clothes on. I tried to send the dog across ahead of me, but at first he refused; finally I got him to go, and, having stripped off my clothes and slung them, stuffed into my fowling bag, across my back, I set off after him. Shivering, teeth chattering, very frightened, I waded out into the water, and by a combination of swimming, dog-paddling and walking through neck-high water, I regained the opposite bank and collapsed exhausted.

However the day was not yet over, nor was the discomfort because I had to make my way back to Strood by pushbike, wet through and bitterly cold. I had nothing on my feet, as my waders were somewhere in the Medway; but at least I was safe. All I had lost was a box of cartridges, my decoys and my waders; I might have lost my life.

I got a few strange looks on the journey home.

LOST WHEELCHAIR

For some years I didn't go shooting because of my multiple sclerosis; I couldn't even hold a cup properly, let alone a gun. Shooting had been one of the great joys in life, and when I couldn't go, I felt devastated. What would I do without my shooting? Then I had a slight remission, and although I was still in a wheelchair, I could at least go fishing. Shortly after, Joe Irving, a gundog trainer from Lockerbie in south-west Scotland, phoned and invited me up to shoot a few clays; I seized on the suggestion and was soon made welcome at Joe's house.

I sat in my wheelchair watching the clays going to and fro, but just couldn't bring myself to shoot. I kept thinking that if I *didn't* try, then at least in my *mind* I could still shoot; but if I tried and failed, how would I cope? Finally I couldn't resist the temptation. 'Pull!' I shouted. Up with the gun and onto the first clay and pull the trigger: thump went the gun, and a clay was busted. On to the second, and I missed. I spent an hour shooting clays, and I was back and once more I could shoot. Many thanks, Joe Irving, for helping me regain the confidence to do so.

The next year I was back into fowling, though only for a couple of trips because I was restricted as to where I could shoot. One December found me on the Solway marshes with brothers Brian and Peter Smith, and we had a good time: Brian had a goose, while Peter and I shot a couple of ducks. Life was good, even if it had to be lived from a wheelchair. Another morning the brothers were dragging me across firm sand to a spot we had picked out the day before, when the wheels of my chair got stuck and the whole chair started to sink: we had hit quicksand. Brian and Peter grabbed me and heaved me clear, and we sat on the mud and watched the chair slowly sink; in no time it was gone. Before we left, we planted a cross made from two pieces of driftwood; and the inscription: RIP, James' wheelchair is buried here.

SCOTTISH GEESE

For fishing and shooting, Scotland has always had a special place in my heart, perhaps because my father hailed from Aberdeen. Many is the time I have looked across the Nith towards Criffel and watched pinkfooted geese moving so high over the marsh that anti-aircraft weapons would be needed to reach them. One trip to this Mecca of fowling was at Christmas. I left the warm fireside on Boxing Day, and headed north through Carlisle and on to Gretna Green where young lovers used to get married; from there it was onto the A75 bound for Annan and goose country. Just past Annan I turned off to the village of Broth Well; there, in Moonflight Cottage, Alicia and Geoff Beesley welcomed me with a pot of tea. For Druid it meant a spot of exercise: this was to be his first goose-hunting trip.

At about 3 p.m. Geoff said, 'Let's get ready for the flight, then'; but I was ready and waiting, fully kitted out for the marsh and armed with a 3-inch magnum 12-bore, and half-a-dozen 3-inch number 3s in my pocket. As we left Moonflight a strong south-westerly was blowing in our faces. Geoff decided we should pitch ourselves in a mud gully at Thaite Burn, hoping to catch the geese as they flighted out to the sands to roost. As dusk approached the pink-foots showed. This English guide who once worked at British Leyland Cowley Works could certainly put you under the geese; skein after skein flighted overhead. However, we didn't fire because they were about five gunshots high, though I could hear some other idiot shooting. Finally in the inky blackness we moved out of our hides and walked slowly back to Moonflight with Geoff's Chesapeake Bay retriever and my Druid at our heels; no action for these two on this flight. In thirty minutes we were back at Broth Well where, it is said, Robert Burns quenched his thirst in 1796. After a shower and some food for dogs and humans, we went off to the local, the Farmers' Inn, where Ian and Margaret Johnson are the perfect hosts and make fowlers welcome and their dogs, too.

Next morning, however, when the alarm rang at 5 a.m. it was a different story, and the wind was howling and rain hammered the windows. I got up, dressed, and had a quick cup of tea and some toast. I pulled on my camou-flaged waterproofs and pocketed a dozen 3-inch magnum number 3s, praying the geese would be low; I had certainly caught goose fever again. This dawn really *was* goose-hunting weather: we opened the door to a fully fledged gale.

From Moonflight to Cockpool, where we hoped to ambush the geese as they left the roosting grounds, was a walk of about twenty minutes. We were there in plenty of time, and I sat hunched up in my hide, seeking what little shelter I could from the driving rain. As first light broke the wind increased in intensity and the flimsy hide shook as if some giant's hand had grabbed it. My excitement rose as I heard the geese calling long before they had come into sight. The music became intense.

Soon there was a skein of about forty pinkfoot geese overhead. Thump, went the 12-bore magnum, and the lead goose staggered as number 3s found their target; it peeled away from the skein like a stricken World War Two bomber; then its wings folded and it crashed to earth 600 yards away. Time for Druid to work, and what a super job he did in retrieving his first goose! He had to cross two fast-flowing streams, and it was a joy to watch him.

A happy pair of fowlers returned to Moonflight for breakfast. When I get a goose – and it doesn't seem to matter how many I have shot before – I'm always on a high for the next twenty-four hours. It's not the number you shoot; it's just being out at dawn and dusk. In fact most goose shooters only take a brace these days.

CHAPTER 7

The Beeb and I

A Poem for Martin James

The riverside is calling me
To spend some time alone,
Mother Nature offering
A place upon her throne,
To be among the cool and green,
And fish with rod and line,
To feel the sun upon my back,
And stop the hands of time.
Casting on the river's flow,
Waiting for his catch,
A kingfisher dives from way above,
His skill is hard to match.
Seeing wildlife scurry by,
Proud to share their home,
The song of birds upon the air,
Myself, but not alone.

Lorraine Davies

For almost twenty years I have been making fishing programmes for the BBC. I have appeared in television and video programmes too, but if I've got the choice it's the wireless for me any day. The first of my radio broadcasts was a series of half-hour programmes called *Hook Line and Sinker* which went out twice weekly; the producer was Simon Johnson, and it was his professionalism which made the programme popular with anglers and non-anglers alike. Simon became a keen angler, and somehow he managed to turn me into an angling broadcaster. The programmes were always made at the waterside, never in the studio, and we tried to cover the very best in angling and countryside matters; I wanted to create a 'Crabtree world' where everything was wonderful.

My fishing guest-list read like a *Who's Who* of angling: it included Richard Walker, Dennis Watkins-Pitchford (BB), Mike Harris, Tag Barnes, Chris Yates, Tony Miles, Bernard Venables, Marsh Pratley, Fred J. Taylor, Bob

James and Robert Atkins, who was the Sports Minister at the time. Then there were those with whom I couldn't fish, but who were with me on the wireless: Maurice Ingham, Chris Tarrent, Bernard Cribbins, Tim Paisley, Hugh Falkus, Allan Edwards, Dick Kefford and many more.

The programme has taken listeners to places in Europe, Canada and North and South America; we have caught coarse, game, sea, and big game fish from a variety of waters. Live on the wireless we have landed some superb fish, from 2lb roach to 20lb salmon, carp and pike.

Another well-known angler who has been on my programme is Brian Moreland of Yorkshire. When I was in my wheelchair, he arranged for part of his syndicate water on the River Ure to be made available to me, and it was there that I caught a 3lb perch on the last day of the 1992–3 season: Brian did all the hard work of finding a shoal of big fish, and then he let me catch them. That's generosity for you!

Nor has sea fishing been neglected: we have gone out on boats from Fleetwood, Dover, Great Yarmouth and many other angling ports, and listeners have heard us boating a 26lb cod, a 21lb thornback ray and a 12lb bass. On a trip from the Isle of Mull, we had three anglers playing 100lb-plus skate, all at the same time.

Then one evening I was fishing for bream and recording my thoughts for my wireless programme when the silver paper bite indicator moved. I struck into a good fish, which turned out to be a bream of 10lb 6oz which had taken a cocktail bait of worm and corn. This was my first and only double-figure bream, and all recorded as it happened while I was in my wheelchair. I was overjoyed with both the fish and the recording.

Apart from angling, I also make programmes on environmental issues and natural history. My Saturday morning programme regularly features the Royal Society for the Protection of Birds, a society which does care about the environment and is not against angling. Listeners to these programmes have heard the sounds of wildlife from the Amazon jungle to the gentle chalk streams of southern England; from the Canadian wilderness to the cultivated vineyards of Bordeaux. The people at BBC Radio Lancashire and Radio 5 have been really helpful, allowing me to record programmes well in advance, because unfortunately there are days when I cannot talk, get dressed or feed myself. And the engineers Bernard, Peter and George have made all sorts of gadgets that enable me to fish and record at the same time.

When Radio 5 first came on the air I had a spell of nineteen months without a break. My morning angling slot was so popular that I even had a fan club, run by a lovely lady called Beryl, from Barkingside in Essex. For me it was great fun. One of the fan club members was Lorraine Davies from Prestatyn in Clwyd, and she and her mother have become close friends of Kate and me. Lorraine has written many lovely poems, several of which have been broadcast on my programmes, and as you have seen, included in this book, too.

Every November the BBC have a Children in Need day, and I always get involved. I ask publishers and tackle firms to donate items for auction, and listeners can bid for early Christmas presents. We raise many hundreds of pounds. Sometimes on Children in Need day I go to Barnsfold trout fishery in Lancashire and catch a few trout which are then auctioned off on the programme; if I don't catch enough, proprietor Frank Casson gives us some out of the cages. One year a lady bid £50 for a brace of trout; I then said that if she would bid another £50 I would go along wearing evening dress and cook them. She did, and it was a fun evening. I didn't leave until around midnight, but it raised a hundred pounds.

On another occasion I offered myself for a day to the highest bidder, and was really flattered when dozens of people entered the bidding. When the price reached £60, seven bidders were left; at £80 there were just two, by which time we were all wondering if we would raise £100. In the end a lady did offer £100, and when the programme was over I phoned her.

'Hello, Mrs Little? Martin James here. You have just bid £100 to spend a day with me. What would you like to do?'

'Oh, *I* didn't want a day with you; it was for my daughter Louise. You are her Christmas present.' A pause . . .

'Er . . . how old is your daughter?'

'Louise is twenty-one and she listens to you every week. My husband and I thought a day with you would be a really good Christmas present.' 'Oh yes,' I thought, 'and that sounds like rather a nice Christmas present for me too!' We agreed that I would turn up on Christmas Day with an invitation for Louise to join me for a day's trout fishing at Barnsfold Water. I hired a Father Christmas outfit, and then a few days before Christmas it was announced on the wireless that if any organization wanted a Santa on Christmas morning, Martin James was available. Lots of people phoned in, and that Christmas morning, with a sack of presents, largely fishing tackle and books, I called in for breakfast at a young mother and baby unit in Preston; then on to an old people's home; and finally to the Little household. I knocked, and Louise opened the door. In a squeaky voice I said, 'Louise Little? Father Christmas has come to see you.'

She said, 'You're not Father Christmas; you're Martin James.' After some hot mince pies and coffee, I went off home feeling that it had been a very good morning.

In April, Louise joined me at Barnsfold Water where Frank Casson gave her some casting instruction; then we went out in a boat with Mike James, who had travelled down from Cumbria to be boatman for the day. (I was recording the event for a future programme.) For lunch we went to the Derby Arms restaurant at Longridge where Louise was our special guest; then it was back to Barnsfold where Louise fished hard. She returned home with a brace of rainbow trout.

On another Children in Need day, June Walker bid £70 to have lunch with me and then join me on the River Ribble to try and catch a chub. This we did in fine style: conditions were perfect, and in a two-hour session we had ten chub averaging 2½lb, which prompted June to say, 'Now I see why you go fishing, Martin, and it's something I would like to take up.' She received a signed photograph of us together; and I hope she is now an avid angler.

Then there was the time when I was asked to switch on the Christmas lights at Torrisholm just outside Lancaster. A few people were gathered around me, asking for autographs, when one lady said, 'How did you get here so quickly from Hampshire? I heard you on the radio at teatime!'

'Oh, that's no problem,' I teased, 'We use helicopters and light aircraft.'

She believed it! 'What a wonderful idea! We're ever so glad you could come to help with our fundraising.' I couldn't bring myself to spoil the illusion, as many listeners really do still think you are live when you are talking on the wireless. The fund-raising was in aid of a specially adapted wheelchair for a little girl, and the cheque I received I gave straight to her wheelchair fund. That's what life is all about: helping those less fortunate than ourselves. Apart from my expenses, all the fees for my talks, slide shows and company promotion activities go to charity.

As I write this book, I am on the wireless from Monday to Friday each evening with *At the Water's Edge*, trying hard to bring the best in angling to listeners young and old. In the course of giving talks to the WI, disabled groups, Lions and so on I generally meet some of my listeners and usually ask what they like about the programmes. Often they say something like, 'Because you make it sound interesting.'

That will do for me!

WHIRLWIND ROMANCE

It is 19 December 1990. I am in my local newsagents, talking about Christmas and how I have been invited to visit France with some friends. The newsagent's son quips, 'D'you want somebody to carry your case?'

Another voice says, 'That's just what I was going to say.'

I look round, and there stands this fair-haired lady.

'Oh, yes? And what would your husband have to say about that?' I ask.

'I haven't got one,' she says. And that was how romance entered my life. When by chance we met again, outside Woolworth's, I gave her my card and said, 'I'm taking my daughter and her boyfriend out for dinner on the twenty-eighth. If you would like to join us, give me a ring the day before.'

The day after Boxing Day I was working at home when the phone rang. 'Hello, it's Kate here. Is that dinner date still on?'

'Yes, of course. But what are you doing tomorrow lunchtime?'

'Nothing special,' Kate told me.

'All right, I'll pick you up at 12.30.' I put the phone down and looked up the number of the Old Post House restaurant in Clitheroe; I booked a table for four, then carried on writing my article for the *Clitheroe Advertiser and Times*.

Kate and I had lunch together, and then dinner that evening with my daughter Sharon and her boyfriend. The next day we went to Blackburn shopping, and then out with friends to a restaurant in Gisburn where the food and service were terrible. Kate and I spent the next two days together. We went back to the Old Post House restaurant in Clitheroe for a special New Year's Eve dinner, and at three minutes past midnight I asked Kate to marry me. She said she would be proud to. It all happened that quickly.

On 9 February we were back at the Old Post House for Kate's birthday and our engagement party, and on 24 August we were married at Trinity Church in Clitheroe. The reception was – yes, you've guessed it – at the Old Post House.

On the morning of the wedding my best man, Nick Millward, and I went trout fishing at Barnsfold Water. Unknown to me, my producer Simon Johnson had arranged with Nick to have a telephone in the boat, and at 9 a.m. it rang. BBC presenter John Briggs said, 'Martin James, you are live on Radio 5. What are you doing fishing? You are supposed to be getting married today!'

It was all good fun, and no doubt the listeners had a chuckle. We caught some nice rainbow trout, and then went ashore for fresh bacon sandwiches. And yes – I did get to the church on time!

Kate and I spent our honeymoon in Florida and Canada fishing, learning to water-ski and making new friends. We had a wonderful time, and Kate caught her first salmon; in fact she was the only one to catch anything that day. She is a super wife: no-one could wish for better. When I'm going through a rough patch she helps me out, pushing my wheelchair about and feeding and dressing me when I can't manage it myself; if I fall over she picks me up and dusts me down; she sorts out fishing spots where we can take the wheelchair. She even fishes in all weathers!

With my Kate, I really hit the jackpot.

PUTTING SOMETHING BACK

Having had to rely on other people for so much help, I try whenever possible to work for the benefit of others. I have organized fishing for children of all ages, and competitions to raise money for those who are infirm and need help twenty-four hours a day. I've been to hell and back myself, and I know what it's like. Currently I am vice-chairman of the Ribble Valley Crossroads Carers, an organization that puts trained help into homes so that carers can have a few hours to themselves. A great number of men and women have to look after wives or husbands, sons or daughters confined to bed because of illness and our aim is to provide help where we can; but it all costs money. Some comes from grants, but much of it we only raise thanks to the generosity of the people of the Ribble Valley.

Each year we organize a coffee morning in the mayor's parlour, which brings in around £500; money from my talks all around the country and from my newspaper and magazine articles also goes to help support Crossroads' valuable work. That, I feel, is what life is about: helping those less fortunate than ourselves.

I am also involved with the Ribble Valley Multiple Sclerosis Society which organizes regular meeting with guest speakers, slide shows, and most important, provides advice and support to people newly diagnosed as having MS. We help one another through the rough periods, because we all have days when our body lets us down.

MOCK MAYOR

I've had many friends who have held the office of mayor, but never for one moment did I expect to be called by that title. In the summer of 1992 I arrived home from France to find a message on my answerphone asking me to call the editor of the *Clitheroe Advertiser and Times*. He asked me if I would consider being the next mock Mayor of Worston. All the proceeds from the mayor-making ceremony go to various charities, so I accepted.

The mayor-making takes place in the grounds of the Calf's Head at Worston, a small village in the Ribble Valley; there, local charities set up their stalls to entertain visitors and raise money. They have drum majorettes, clowns, a magician; you can have a go at 'catch the ferret', and there is a fly dresser who ties and sells fishing flies. Everyone dresses up in medieval costume, and in the pub there are serving wenches in attendance.

A cold north-easterly wind was blowing on our mayor-making day, and the weatherman had promised rain; not ideal conditions to encourage people to leave their homes. But they did, and it stayed fine. 1993 was the 400th birthday of Izaak Walton, the author of *The Compleate Angler*, so I dressed as Izaak would have; I also had a cane fishing pole with a horse-hair line, which proved quite an attraction. At 4 o'clock the town crier shouted 'Oyez, oyez, oyez! Now is the time to install the new mayor of Worston, Mr Martin James, angler and broadcaster.' And with six of the previous mayors in attendance, the outgoing mayor, John Barry, installed me as mayor. Then it was time to count the money and pack everything away for the following year.

From this fun day we raised £3,000 for charity. As the theme for my year in office I chose children and the environment.

STUCK FOR WORDS

I have received awards from many quarters, and I cherish these dearly. I have long been an active supporter of the Anglers' Cooperative Association, angling's pollution-fighting body and an active organization to which I feel every thinking angler should belong. For me, a high point of the eighties was when I received an illuminated scroll from the ACA for my work in trying to improve the environment; Lord Mason of Barnsley presented me with the award in Fishmongers' Hall, in London.

But the award I value above all others I received on Saturday 3 April 1993. I had just given a presentation on fly fishing for pike at a conference of the National Association of Specialist Anglers in Loughborough, and was about to leave the stage when I was asked to sit down for a minute; I thought perhaps it was so that help could be arranged to get me out of the conference hall. Then Marsh Pratley, the conference organizer, walked onto the rostrum carrying a bronze bust of Richard Walker. I had seen one before in 1982, when it had been awarded to the Anglers' Cooperative Association.

Chairman Phil Smith asked for silence and said a few words about the trophy, and then announced *me* as being the recipient. I was dumb-struck. Tears rolled down my cheeks when I was presented with that magnificent trophy.

After some time, during which Phil Smith told the assembly, 'We've got Martin James speechless, for the very first time!' I composed myself and thanked everyone.

The Richard Walker trophy is the most beautiful thing I could wish for. Thank you, everyone. I shall treasure it for the rest of my days.

The Crossroads Story

Many people still remember Crossroads, the television serial about a family who ran a Birmingham motel. What is less well known is that the serial and the Crossroads respite care service for carers are connected. This came about because Sandy Richardson, the son of Meg the motel owner, had a car accident; as a result, when he returned home he was temporarily paralysed. Later another character, Tony Scott, a young physically disabled man being cared for at home by his mother Helen, was written into the script. But, as with so many relatives and carers in this situation, the right type of help was not available at the right time.

The storyline for this character was modelled on the real-life story of Noel Crane, a young man who had broken his neck in a diving accident. When he returned home he was looked after by his mother, who bore all the stresses of a caring relative. The suggestion put forward in the programme was to find a helper to take over and give the caring relative some respite. The result was a deluge of letters from viewers who asked why such a service could not be provided. In 1974 Associated Television responded by providing £10,000 for a two-year pilot project to be set up which would adapt the fictional idea and translate it into a real-life scheme to provide help for those who cared for disabled people in their homes. Rugby was chosen as the town for the pilot because it was not too large and was also surrounded by rural communities. The project was named the Crossroads Care Attendant Scheme because of its links with the TV series, and Noel Crane and his mother were among the first families to receive help from a Crossroads care attendant.

Success Story

That was back in 1974. The pilot project was so successful that by 1978 there were twelve such programmes running. The 100th Crossroads scheme, Derwent and Wye, was launched in 1987 and the 200th, Wigan and Leigh, joined the Crossroads National Association in 1992. Today the Crossroads network covers England, Scotland, Wales and Northern Ireland, and there are now six schemes running in Holland. As I write, there are 225 schemes in operation and our target is to achieve 250 by 1995, which will be Crossroads' twenty-first Anniversary. The first scheme employed five care attendants and helped 28 families. Today 2,700 care attendants support 22,000 families. The annual cost of running the service is £14,000,000.

Crossroads enjoys tremendous support. The national patrons are The Baroness Masham of Ilton, The Rt Hon the Lord Ashley of Stoke, Sir Roy Griffiths, The Rt Hon Alfred Morris MP, Mrs Norma Major, Leonard Mathews OBE, with Norman Banner, a former chairman of Crossroads National Association, as President.

There are nearly seven million people in the UK caring for someone who is dependent upon them because of illness or disability. By the year 2000 one in five people will be looking after a spouse, child, parent or friend who will require constant support. Many carers are struggling to remain in work – in fact 22 per cent of the families who received Crossroads help last year were in that position. Of growing concern is the number of young people who are looking after a sick or disabled relative; many caring for single parents. Crossroads has evidence of some very young children acting in a caring role. Carers tend to have low expectations, as they put the disabled person first. But these young people are the future of the nation and they deserve to be able to grasp a wide variety of experiences if they are to develop as individuals. The essence of Crossroads is to care about carers and to bring them relief. Should this be such a luxury?

Much has been achieved since that first pilot scheme in Rugby, but there is still much more to do. Crossroads schemes employ their staff and train them in all aspects of basic nursing care: lifting and handling, first aid, specific disabilities and of course the particular problems and needs of carers and disabled people. With Crossroads support a carer can confidently take a break knowing that there is someone reliable and competent at home to care for their disabled relative, listening to their worries with complete confidentiality.

Crossroads in our Valley

The Ribble Valley scheme that I am involved with was launched in 1988. Like the first scheme in Rugby it employed just five care attendants; now there are eleven. Each scheme has a voluntary management committee who offer help and expertise free of charge, not even claiming expenses. The management committee of Ribble Valley Crossroads is made up of representatives from the Health Authority, a G.P., members of the local business community, disabled people and carers themselves; and we are fortunate to have Lady Clitheroe as our President. Local schemes can respond to local needs and yet be part of the overall regional and national structure of Crossroads.

118

The Ribble Valley scheme is currently providing help to some 65 families spanning all age groups and all disabilities, including the terminally ill. We cover a beautiful rural area of some 224 square miles in north-east Lancashire with a population of some 53,000. The rural nature of the area brings its own problems: carers often face transport difficulties; they need more time to get to shops or to other activities; and the cost per Crossroads care hour is also higher because of mileage. Sometimes in winter our care attendants have to follow the snowplough to reach someone and give them the care they so urgently need. But there are compensations: the wonderful, ever changing scenery, the people and the positive community support for our work far outweigh the difficulties.

Funding for the Ribble Valley scheme comes mainly from Social Services. However, grants from the Rural Development Commission, from the B.B.C. Children-in-Need appeal, and from Granada's Telethon, as well as community fund raising and financial support from the carers and families themselves, have helped the service to grow and develop. My contribution has been to give to Crossroads the proceeds from many of my talks and slide shows around the country and the fees from my magazine articles. To this I am adding the royalties from this book.

All this has meant that as well as receiving regular day to day help, carers have also been able to attend weddings, christenings and family parties and have the occasional special day out – things the rest of us take for granted. But most important of all, this service remains free of charge to the carers.

A Special Kind of Help

Crossroads is a very confidential service and therefore specific details of the care cannot be given; however, the following examples are typical of the help which Crossroads offers:

- To look after a disabled lady whilst her husband goes with his son to each home match of his local football team.
- To get up, wash and dress daily a very elderly lady who lives with her daughter who has recently had a severe traffic accident.
- To take over from a carer who has to look after her paralysed son twenty-four hours a day; she is now able to have a part-time job and the occasional evening out with her husband.
- To help the mother of a young family of four children including a girl with dual disabilities, so that they can all go out together, or so that the mother can take out the other three while the Crossroads care attendant attends to the needs of the young disabled girl.

Much has grown out of that first pilot scheme in Rugby, but we all know that much more still needs to be done. I know how important the scheme is to the carers, because I have a carer – my wife – and if the day should ever come when I need round-the-clock care then at least I will know that there will be someone to give my wife a break and take over caring for me.

If you would like to help the Crossroads movement, or if you know someone who needs their help, you can obtain details of your nearest branch from:

National Association of Crossroads Care Attendants Schemes
10 Regent Place
Rugby
Warwickshire CV21 2PN
Tel: 0788 573653